LISTS TO LIVE BY

"*Lists to Live By* is sometimes humorous, often thought-provoking, and always practical and inspiring. At a time when most of us live by our daily 'to-do' lists, this book reminds us how 'to-be.'"

—NANCY STAFFORD
Actress / author

"Every home will be blessed to have a copy of this extraordinary book, *Lists to Live By*, in its library. Any question you might have about living in our fast-paced world can be answered thanks to an easy-reference style and wise, practical advice and counsel.

"You will find each list in this marvelous book a key to living a successful, happy life. Here is the invaluable advice that we need for ourselves as well as a resource to guide our children. This book will change your life if you apply these insightful lists...they will bring order, peace, and love!

"Read it, use it, share it, live by it...you'll live a better life."

—KEN WALES
Executive producer,
CBS television series "Christy"; author / speaker

LISTS TO LIVE BY: THE SECOND COLLECTION
published by Multnomah Publishers, Inc.

© 2001 by Alice Gray, Steve Stephens, John Van Diest
International Standard Book Number: 1-57673-685-7

The lists in this book are not substitutes for obtaining professional advice from qualified persons and organizations. Consult the appropriate professional advisor for complete and updated information.

Every effort has been made to provide proper and accurate source attributions for selections in this volume. If any attribution is incorrect, the publisher welcomes written documentation supporting correction for subsequent printings. The publisher gratefully acknowledges the cooperation of publishers and individuals granting permission for use of selections. Please see the acknowledgments for full attribution of these sources.

Scripture quotations are from:
The Living Bible © 1971. Used by permission of Tyndale House Publishers, Inc.
All rights reserved.

For information:
MULTNOMAH PUBLISHERS, INC.
POST OFFICE BOX 1720
SISTERS, OREGON 97759

Library of Congress Cataloging-in-Publication Data:

Lists to live by: the second collection / compiled by Alice Gray, Steve Stephens,
John Van Diest.
    p. cm.
Originally published: Sisters, Or.: Multnomah Publishers, 1999.
Includes bibliographical references.
  ISBN 1-57673-685-7
  1.Conduct of life—Handbooks, manuals, etc. 2. Life skills—Handbooks, manuals, etc.
I. Gray, Alice, 1939– II. Stephens, Steve. III. Van Diest, John.
BJ1581.2.L55 2001
646.7—dc21

                                    00-011543

01 02 03 04 05 06 07 08 — 10 9 8 7 6 5 4 3 2

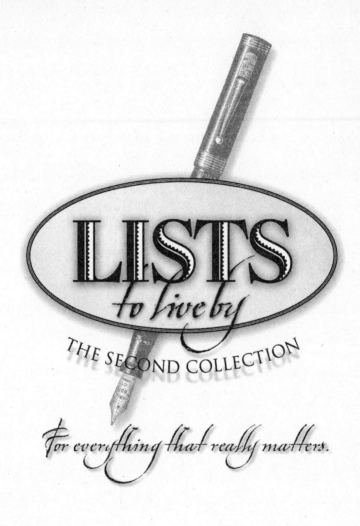

LISTS
to live by

THE SECOND COLLECTION

For everything that really matters.

COMPILED BY

ALICE GRAY, STEVE STEPHENS, AND JOHN VAN DIEST

Multnomah® Publishers *Sisters, Oregon*

CONTENTS

PEOPLE LOVE LISTS!

LISTS ARE...

- *short*
- *to the point*
- *neat and tidy*
- *easy to read*
- *hard to forget*
- *and you can live your life by them!*

Throughout history, people have had lists. From Moses to Mother Teresa to Colin Powell, lists have helped people to prioritize life and bring into focus what is of greatest value.

Reading a single list is like having the best parts of a whole book gathered into a few words. Huge truths wrapped in small packages. In this second collection of Lists to Live By, you have a virtual library of information at your fingertips.

One wise sage said, "The book of life is lived in chapters, so know your page number." But as life gets more cluttered with too many things, too many activities, and even too many words...perhaps instead of page numbers, we should know our lists—lists about wisdom, contentment, success, health, marriage, family, friends, and virtue. These are the things that really matter...and they are all here in this book, just waiting for you to discover them.

ALICE GRAY   DR. STEVE STEPHENS   JOHN VAN DIEST

SUCCESS

Growing through learning and creativity

1

SEVEN FAVORITE QUOTATIONS
OF ZIG ZIGLAR

1.
Happiness is not a when or a where, but a here and a now!

2.
When you associate with winners, your chances of winning go up!

3.
You don't have to be great to start, but you have to start to be great.

4.
If you aren't on fire, then your wood is wet.

5.
I'm not going to ease up, slow up, or give up until I'm taken up.

6.
You don't drown by falling into water. You only drown if you stay there.

7.
You can have everything you want
if you help enough other people get what they want.

ZIG ZIGLAR
AUTHOR OF "I'LL SEE YOU AT THE TOP"
FROM "CHRISTIAN READER" MAGAZINE

PERSISTENCE

Realize that failure does not mean you should quit.

A test is not a signal to give up.

In every failure, God plants a seed of success.

Never blame others for your lack of success.

CHARLES STANLEY
FROM "IN TOUCH" MAGAZINE

THREE GREAT ESSENTIALS

THREE ESSENTIALS FOR ACHIEVING
ANYTHING WORTHWHILE:

1.
Hard work

2.
Stick-to-itiveness

3.
Common sense

THOMAS EDISON
INVENTOR

20 POWER THOUGHTS

1.

Curiosity leads to creativity.

2.

Trust your positive instincts.

3.

When it's dark, look for the stars.

4.

Faith is always stronger than failure.

5.

Build a dream and the dream builds you.

6.

Obstacles are opportunities in disguise.

7.

When the going gets tough—laugh.

8.

Don't miss the best things in life.

9.

Itemize your assets.

10.

Fix the problem, not the blame.

11.

Share the credit.

12.
Never make an irreversible decision in a down time.

13.
Treasure time like gold.

14.
Never judge reality by your limited experiences.

15.
You will never win if you never begin.

16.
Success without conflict is unrealistic.

17.
Make sure your dreams are big enough for God to fit in.

18.
Never let a problem become an excuse.

19.
*When it looks like you've exhausted all possibilities,
remember this: you haven't.*

20.
Always look at what you have left. Never look at what you have lost.

ROBERT H. SCHULLER
FROM "POWER THOUGHTS"

THE TRUE MEASURE OF SUCCESS

To be able to carry money without spending it;

To be able to bear an injustice without retaliating;

To be able to do one's duty when critical eyes watch;

To be able to keep at a job until it is finished;

To be able to do the work and let others receive the recognition;

To be able to accept criticism without letting it whip you;

To like those who push you down;

To love when hate is all about you;

To follow God when others put detour signs in your path;

To have a peace of heart and mind because you have given God your best;

This is the true measure of success.

AUTHOR UNKNOWN

LADDER OF SUCCESS

Plan purposefully.

Prepare prayerfully.

Proceed positively.

Pursue persistently.

AFRICAN-AMERICAN PROVERB

PEOPLE WHO MAKE A DIFFERENCE HAVE...

INITIATIVE — *being a self-starter with contagious energy.*

VISION — *seeing beyond the obvious, claiming new objectives.*

UNSELFISHNESS — *releasing the controls and the glory.*

TEAMWORK — *involving, encouraging, and supporting others.*

FAITHFULNESS — *hanging in there in season and out.*

ENTHUSIASM — *providing affirmation, excitement to the task.*

DISCIPLINE — *modeling great character regardless of the odds.*

CONFIDENCE — *representing security, faith, and determination.*

CHARLES R. SWINDOLL
FROM "THE FINISHING TOUCH"

THOUGHTS THAT HOLD US BACK

I can't

That's a problem

That's not fair

I won't

It's been tried before

Never

Stupid

It won't work

It's too hard

Impossible

It's hopeless

I'm not good enough

Hate

I'll get even

JOHN VAN DIEST
ASSOCIATE PUBLISHER

EFFECTIVE LEADERS

1.
EFFECTIVE LEADERS LISTEN

If we do not hear what is said to us, our leadership will be impertinent.

2.
EFFECTIVE LEADERS HAVE VISION

A leader charts a course, navigates difficult places,
and sets an example.

3.
EFFECTIVE LEADERS ARE PASSIONATE

They have a passion for their role, their task, and their partners.

4.
EFFECTIVE LEADERS ARE FACILITATORS

Leaders do not shelter those they care for from the harsh realities of life.
They facilitate the ability of others to live passionate lives.

5.
EFFECTIVE LEADERS EMPOWER

This will occur as you talk with them [those who follow], share your
struggles with them, convey your convictions, declare your doubts,
and tell them about the difficulties you are experiencing.

PRESTON GILLHAM
CONDENSED FROM "THINGS ONLY MEN KNOW"

DON'TS FOR DECISION MAKING

Don't focus on doing *more* tasks, but on doing *fewer* tasks well.

Don't accept impossible deadlines—factor in extra "pad" time.

Don't leave decisions hanging—decide immediately on a course of action each time you can.

Don't let the desires of others dictate how you spend your time.

Don't assume that the "emergencies" of others are your emergencies.

Don't say *yes* when you should say *no*.

JUNE HUNT
FROM "HEALING THE HURTING HEART"

ARE YOU A GOOD TIME MANAGER?

DO YOU
have a clear picture of what you want to accomplish each day?

DO YOU
list tasks and appointments on your calendar?

DO YOU
have a few clear goals for each activity and project you're involved in?

DO YOU
group similar tasks together to do at the same time?

DO YOU
feel free not to read everything that crosses your desk?

DO YOU
*balance your time on projects so you don't require
frenzied hours of overtime to finish?*

DO YOU
prioritize your tasks in order and stick to top-priority items?

DO YOU
*keep important references and supplies within
arm's reach of your work area?*

DO YOU
*give clear instructions to coworkers so they can take care of
minor jobs without interrupting you?*

DO YOU
work on highly involved tasks when you feel the most alert?

DO YOU
stop working when you feel fatigued?

DO YOU
*break large projects down into manageable
pieces to finish one at a time?*

DO YOU
survey your long-term goals regularly?

ALICE GRAY, DR. STEVE STEPHENS, AND JOHN VAN DIEST

SMART GOALS ARE...

SPECIFIC

MEASURABLE

ACHIEVABLE

REALISTIC

TIMED

ALICE GRAY, DR. STEVE STEPHENS, AND JOHN VAN DIEST

CRITICISM KILLS...

❧

MOTIVATION

❧

ENTHUSIASM

❧

CONFIDENCE

❧

JOY

❧

DREAMS

❧

HOPE

❧

SPIRIT

❦

DR. STEVE STEPHENS
PSYCHOLOGIST AND SEMINAR SPEAKER

SUCCESS

SIX-STEP RECIPE FOR SUCCESS

1.
BE PASSIONATE.
Love what you do.

2.
THE GREATEST WEALTH IS FAMILY AND FRIENDS.
Enjoy their love.

3.
EVERY DAY IS SPECIAL.
Make it the best it can be.

4.
"NO" IS UNACCEPTABLE.
Don't stop there. Go for "yes."

5.
CELEBRATE EXCELLENCE.
Make people feel important.

6.
THE GREATEST FAILURE IS NOT TO TRY.
When you dream, wake up and do.

JEFFREY GITOMER
FROM "WOMEN AS MANAGERS"

FIVE KEYS TO CONVERSATION

1.
STAND UP STRAIGHT, LOOK THEM IN THE EYE, AND SMILE

A warm, confident greeting communicates acceptance and responsibility.

2.
RESPOND WITH CONFIDENCE—DON'T MUTTER

When we meet a person who has the confidence to speak to us clearly with sparkling eyes and a warm grin, we immediately connect with them.

3.
LEARN PEOPLE'S NAMES AND USE THEIR NAMES PROPERLY

Learning to use people's names with respect and courtesy is fundamental to basic conversation.

4.
DEVELOP A GENERAL KNOWLEDGE BASE

Versatility in conversation is invaluable. With a general understanding of politics, entertainment, sports, and religion you'll be amazed at the depth of conversation and friendships that will emerge.

5.
FOCUS ON THE OTHER PERSON

Many people fail at conversation simply because they are too interested in fronting their own point of view. They don't want to talk to someone—they want to talk at someone.

TED HAGGARD AND JOHN BOLIN
CONDENSED FROM "CONFIDENT PARENTS, EXCEPTIONAL TEENS"

THE TEN COMMANDMENTS
OF GIVING A SPEECH

1.
THOU SHALT NOT BE UNPREPARED.

Be so familiar with your material that you are not dependent on your notes or your manuscript.

2.
THOU SHALT NOT HAVE ONE METHOD OF GIVING A SPEECH.

Be careful to fit your methodology to your audience.

3.
THOU SHALT NOT CONCENTRATE ON THYSELF.

If you are totally concentrated on yourself, you will miss the whole reason for your speech: communicating something important to an audience.

4.
THOU SHALT NOT MAKE LONG SPEECHES.

The longer the speech, the greater chance of failure.

5.
THOU SHALT NOT LISTEN TO EVERYONE'S CRITICISM.

Find someone you trust and ask that person to give you honest criticism. It will be worth the comments of a thousand others.

6.
THOU SHALT NOT MUMBLE.

Speaking clearly is prerequisite to an audience hearing clearly.

7.
THOU SHALT BE THYSELF.

Be the best you can within your own style and gifts.

8.
THOU SHALT SPEAK GENTLY.

Wise communicators turn down the volume.
They should communicate "Can we talk?" rather than
"This is the law and you will obey."

9.
THOU SHALT WATCH BODY LANGUAGE.

In communication, body language is almost as important as the
words you speak.

10.
THOU SHALT DEVIATE.

Variety is the spice of life and the stuff of a good speech.

STEVE BROWN, PRESIDENT OF KEY LIFE NETWORK, INC.
CONDENSED FROM "HOW TO TALK SO PEOPLE WILL LISTEN"

STEPPING FORWARD

Changing through the seasons of life

2

THREE PILLARS OF LEARNING

1.

Seeing much.

2.

Suffering much.

3.

Studying much.

BENJAMIN DISRAELI
FORMER PRIME MINISTER OF ISRAEL

ONE STEP FURTHER

Do more than exist LIVE

Do more than touch FEEL

Do more than look OBSERVE

Do more than read ABSORB

Do more than hear LISTEN

Do more than listen UNDERSTAND

Do more than think REFLECT

Do more than just talk SAY SOMETHING

AUTHOR UNKNOWN

WANTED!

More to *improve*
    and fewer to *disapprove*.

More *doers*
    and fewer *talkers*.

More to say *It can be done*
    and fewer to say *It's impossible*.

More to *inspire* others
    and fewer to *throw cold water* on them.

More to *get into the thick of things*
    and fewer to *sit on the sidelines*.

More to point out *what's right*
    and fewer to *show what's wrong*.

More to *light a candle*
    and fewer to *curse the darkness*.

AUTHOR UNKNOWN

SEVEN LESSONS TO LEARN

1. LEARN TO
   respect and esteem others.

2. LEARN TO
   *maximize your strengths and
   minimize your weaknesses.*

3. LEARN TO
   be an encourager.

4. LEARN TO
   be friendly.

5. LEARN TO
   approach life with joy and hope.

6. LEARN TO
   forgive.

7. LEARN TO
   treat children special.

JOHN VAN DIEST
ASSOCIATE PUBLISHER

SEVEN IMPORTANT CHOICES

1. CHOOSE
    a goal.

2. CHOOSE
    to use wisdom.

3. CHOOSE
    *how you will
    spend your time.*

4. CHOOSE
    your battles.

5. CHOOSE
    your words.

6. CHOOSE
    your friends.

7. CHOOSE
    your attitude.

SHERI ROSE SHEPHERD
FROM "7 WAYS TO A BETTER YOU"

LIVING LIKE THERE'S NO TOMORROW

IF TODAY WERE THE LAST OF ALL DAYS, WOULD YOU:

- Start the business you have always wanted to?
- Take that special trip you had always planned?
- Heal an old hurt?
- Forgive an old offense?
- Visit someone who would love to see you?
- Reconnect and catch up with an old friend?
- See a sight you have always dreamed of seeing?
- Learn how to do something new?
- Go on an adventure?
- Ask someone to forgive you?
- Learn how to communicate with your spouse?
- Learn how to communicate with your kids?
- Learn how to communicate with your parents?
- Make love with your spouse like you mean it?
- Tell someone how much you love him or her?
- See a movie or read a book?
- Quit sweating the small stuff?
- Finally get it that it's almost all small stuff?

- § Tell someone how much you appreciate what he or she has contributed to your life?

- § Thank someone for believing in you?

- § Gather your family members around you and just hold them?

- § Get your priorities in order?

- § Finish that project you left hanging?

- § Consider what the meaning of your life has been?

- § Focus on what's important?

- § Balance your family and work life?

- § Get to know your kids?

- § Get to know your spouse?

- § Get to know yourself?

- § Let someone in front of you in traffic?

- § Find out the names of the people who live next door, across the street, behind you?

- § Slow down and enjoy what you have worked so hard for?

JEFF HERRING
FROM THE "OREGONIAN"

SEVEN WAYS TO MAKE YOURSELF MISERABLE

1. Count your troubles, name them one by one—at the breakfast table, if anybody will listen, or as soon as possible thereafter.

2. Worry every day about something. Don't let yourself get out of practice.

3. Pity yourself. If you do enough of this, nobody else will have to do it for you.

4. Make it your business to find out what the Joneses are buying this year and where they're going. Try to do them at least one better even if you have to take out another loan.

5. Stay away from absolutes. It's what's right for *you* that matters. Be your own person and don't allow yourself to get hung up on what others expect of you.

6. Make sure you get your rights. Never mind other people's. You have your life to live, they have theirs.

7. Don't fall into any compassion traps—the sort of situation where people can walk all over you. If you get too involved in other people's troubles, you may neglect your own.

ELISABETH ELLIOT
CONDENSED FROM "KEEP A QUIET HEART"

RULES FOR A PERFECT DAY

JUST FOR TODAY I will try to strengthen my mind by reading something that requires effort, thought, and concentration.

JUST FOR TODAY I will do somebody a good turn and not get found out.

JUST FOR TODAY I will do a task that needs to be done but which I have been putting off. I will do it as an exercise in willpower.

JUST FOR TODAY I will dress as becomingly as possible, talk low, act courteously, be liberal with praise, and criticize not one bit nor find fault with anything.

JUST FOR TODAY I will have a quiet half hour all by myself and relax. In this half hour sometime I will think of God so as to get more perspective in my life.

JUST FOR TODAY I will be unafraid. Especially, I will not be afraid to be happy, to enjoy what is beautiful, to love, and to believe that those I love, love me.

AUTHOR UNKNOWN

LIFE 101

I'M LEARNING...

    §   that a good sense of humor is money in the bank. In life. On the job. In a marriage.

    §   that a good attitude can control situations you can't. That any bad experience can be a good one. It all depends on me.

    §   to slow down more often and enjoy the trip. To eat more ice cream and less bran.

    §   that you can do something in an instant that will give you heartache for life.

    §   that bitterness and gossip accomplish nothing, but forgiveness and love accomplish everything.

    §   that it takes years to build trust and seconds to destroy it.

    §   to always leave loved ones with loving words. It may be the last time I see them.

    §   that if I'm standing on the edge of a cliff, the best way forward is to back up. That you don't fail when you lose, you fail when you quit.

    §   that too many people spend a lifetime stealing time from those who love them most, trying to please the ones who care about them the least.

    §   that money is a lousy way of keeping score. That true success is not measured in cars, or homes, or bank accounts, but in relationships.

❧ that having enough money isn't nearly as much fun as I thought it would be when I didn't have any. That money buys less than you think.

❧ that helping another is far more rewarding than helping myself. That those who laugh more worry less.

❧ that you cannot make anyone love you. But you can work on being lovable.

❧ that degrees, credentials, and awards mean far less than I thought they would.

❧ that I will never regret a moment spent reading the Bible or praying. Or a kind word. Or a day at the beach.

❧ that laughter and tears are nothing to be ashamed of. To celebrate the good things. And pray about the bad.

❧ And I'm learning that the most important thing in the world is loving God. That everything good comes from that.

PHIL CALLAWAY
CONDENSED FROM "WHO PUT THE SKUNK IN THE TRUNK?"

GOALS FOR AUTHENTIC GROWTH

I WILL   *have a passion for excellence.*

I WILL   *ask, listen, and hear—to determine the wants, needs, and possibilities of all with whom I come in contact.*

I WILL   *provide an example of commitment and integrity.*

I WILL   *follow a path of continual empowerment for myself and others.*

I WILL   *constantly focus on the strengths of all with whom I come in contact.*

I WILL   *cultivate optimum physical, mental, and spiritual fitness.*

I WILL   *lead as I would like to be led.*

I WILL   *savor the flavor of each passing moment.*

I WILL   *infuse every thought and relationship with faith, hope, love, and gratitude.*

JOE D. BATTEN
FROM "NEW MAN" MAGAZINE

FIVE WAYS TO START
THE NEW YEAR RIGHT

1.
DON'T MAKE RESOLUTIONS.
Make plans. Resolutions are pie-in-the-sky, down-the-road goals.
Plans are doable, step-by-step.

2.
TURN THE TV OFF.
Think how much time you could have to accomplish dreams if
you used even the daily half hour you normally watch TV.

3.
LEARN TO SAY NO.
Prioritize instead of becoming overwhelmed with all your to-dos and
opportunities. Include time for rest/recreation and time for meditation.

4.
WRITE THANK-YOU NOTES FOR SIMPLE REASONS.
Gratitude is a priceless gift, so give it freely!

5.
PRAY ABOUT EVERYTHING.
Talk to God about everyday details, as well as big-picture items.
Nothing is too small—or too big—for Him to care about.

LITA FORSYTH
FROM "VIRTUE" MAGAZINE

FOUR TRAITS OF THOSE
WHO IMPACT OUR LIVES

1. CONSISTENCY.

Those who impact lives stay at the task with reliable regularity. They seem unaffected by the fickle winds of change.

2. AUTHENTICITY.

People who impact others are real to the core; no alloy covered over with a brittle layer of chrome, but solid, genuine stuff right down to the nubbies.

3. UNSELFISHNESS.

Those who impact us the most watch out for themselves the least. They notice our needs and reach out to help, honestly concerned about our welfare. Their least-used words are "I," "me," "my," and "mine."

4. TIRELESSNESS.

With relentless determination they spend themselves. They refuse to quit. Possessing an enormous amount of enthusiasm for their labor, they press on regardless of the odds.

CHARLES R. SWINDOLL
CONDENSED FROM "GROWING STRONG IN THE SEASONS OF LIFE"

WHAT IS MATURITY?

1. Facing the truth honestly.

2. Looking beyond personal comfort and gratification, to the greater good.

3. Dealing with change without falling apart.

4. Working hard and completing a job, whether supervised or not.

5. Keeping the stresses and worries of life from taking control.

6. Doing the right thing regardless of what others say and do.

7. Finding more joy in giving than receiving.

8. Bearing an injustice without having to get even.

9. Relating to others in a consistently positive and helpful manner.

10. Being a person of your word.

11. Demonstrating respect.

12. Showing love in both word and deed.

13. Learning to be content based upon internal attitudes rather than external circumstances.

DR. STEVE STEPHENS
PSYCHOLOGIST AND SEMINAR SPEAKER

VITAL QUESTIONS

Ask yourself:
>What are the options?
>>What are my priorities?
>>>How can I grow?

Ask others:
>Will you forgive me?
>>Will you help me?
>>>What can I do for you?

Ask God:
>Who am I?
>>What is Your will?
>>>What is eternal?

DAVID SANFORD
DIRECTOR OF PRINT MEDIA, LUIS PALAU EVANGELISTIC ASSOCIATION

HOW TO PUT A WOW IN EVERY TOMORROW

DEVELOP AN ATTITUDE OF GRATITUDE.
Even when you are experiencing tough times, remember the blessings in your life.
It's like sprinkling sunshine on a cloudy day.

ENCOURAGE OTHERS.
When someone has a goal, most people point out the obstacles.
You be the one to point out the possibilities.

GIVE SINCERE COMPLIMENTS.
We all like to be remembered for our best moments.

KEEP GROWING.
Walk a different path. Take a class. Read something inspiring.

GIVE THE GIFT OF FORGIVENESS.
Forgiveness is a blessing for the one who forgives
as well as for the one who is forgiven.

TAKE CARE OF YOURSELF.
Exercise, eat a healthy diet, sing, and dance a little bit every day.

DO RANDOM ACTS OF KINDNESS.
The most fun is when the other person doesn't know who did it.

TREASURE RELATIONSHIPS.
Eat meals together, take walks, listen. Share laughter and tears. Make memories.

SHARE YOUR FAITH.
You can wish someone joy and peace and happy things,
but when you share your faith—you've wished them everything.

ALICE GRAY
INSPIRATIONAL CONFERENCE SPEAKER
FROM HER SEMINAR, "TREASURES OF THE HEART"

WE ARE SHAPED BY...

Friends.

Literature.

Music.

Pleasures.

Ambitions.

Thoughts.

A. W. TOZER
FROM "THE QUOTABLE TOZER"

HOW TO LIGHTEN UP

Don't take yourself so seriously.

Thank God for the little things.

Look for an opportunity to help other people.

Choose joy.

Look for the silver lining in every grey cloud.

Add humor to conflicts and difficulties.

Don't base happiness on outward circumstances.

Don't try to be perfect.

Don't be easily offended.

Laugh every chance you get.

KEN DAVIS, COMEDIAN
ADAPTED FROM "LIGHTEN UP".

THE OPTIMIST CREED

COMMIT YOURSELF:

To be so strong that nothing can disturb your peace of mind.

To talk health, happiness, and prosperity to every person you meet.

To make all your friends feel that there is something special in them.

To look at the sunny side of everything and make your optimism come true.

To think only of the best, to work only for the best, and to expect only the best.

To be just as enthusiastic about the success of others as you are about your own.

To forget the mistakes of the past and press on to the greater achievements of the future.

To wear a cheerful countenance at all times and give every living creature you meet a smile.

To give so much time to the improvement of yourself that you have no time to criticize others.

To be too large for worry, too noble for anger, too strong for fear, and too happy to permit the presence of trouble.

OPTIMIST INTERNATIONAL

VIRTUE
Marks of character and quality

3

GREAT SAYINGS ON VIRTUE

I am nothing, but truth is everything.
ABRAHAM LINCOLN

We are shaped and fashioned by what we love.
GOETHE

Integrity without knowledge is weak and useless,
and knowledge without integrity is dangerous and dreadful.
SAMUEL JOHNSON

Always do right—this will gratify some and astonish the rest.
MARK TWAIN

How sweet it is when the strong are also gentle.
LIGGIE FUDIM

Resolved: never to do anything which I should be
afraid to do if it were the last hour of my life.
JONATHAN EDWARDS

A BALANCED LIFE

SELF-RELIANT   but not Self-sufficient

STEADFAST   but not Stubborn

TACTFUL   but not Timid

SERIOUS   but not Sullen

UNMOVABLE   but not Stationary

GENTLE   but not Hypersensitive

TENDERHEARTED   but not Touchy

CONSCIENTIOUS   but not Perfectionistic

DISCIPLINED   but not Demanding

GENEROUS · but not Gullible

MEEK but not Weak

HUMOROUS but not Hilarious

FRIENDLY but not Familiar

HOLY but not Holier-than-thou

DISCERNING but not Critical

PROGRESSIVE but not Pretentious

AUTHORITATIVE but not Autocratic

FROM "GOD'S LITTLE DEVOTIONAL BOOK"

CHARACTER AND CONDUCT

Conduct is what we do; *character is what we are.*

Conduct is the outward life; *character is the life unseen, hidden within, yet evidenced by that which is seen.*

Conduct is external, seen from without; *character is internal—operating within.*

Character is the state of the heart; **conduct** is its outward expression.

Character is the root of the tree; **conduct,** the fruit it bears.

E. M. BOUNDS
THEOLOGIAN

GOOD CHARACTER IS...

- Showing LOVE when those around are not lovable.

- Having JOY when those around are discouraged and discontent.

- Exuding PEACE when those around are anxious.

- Practicing PATIENCE when those around are hurried and frantic.

- Reaching out in KINDNESS when those around are difficult.

- Shining with GOODNESS when those around do evil.

- Standing in FAITHFULNESS when those around have no commitment.

- Flowing with GENTLENESS when those around are harsh and cruel.

- Demonstrating SELF-CONTROL when those around have none.

BASED ON THE TEACHINGS OF ST. PAUL, THE APOSTLE

VIRTUE

100 POSITIVE VIRTUES

1. Accepting 2. Agreeable 3. Ambitious 4. Appreciative 5. Attentive 6. Available 7. Brave 8. Calm 9. Caring 10. Cheerful 11. Clean 12. Clever 13. Committed 14. Compassionate 15. Concerned 16. Conscientious 17. Considerate 18. Consistent 19. Content 20. Cooperative 21. Courteous 22. Curious 23. Dependable 24. Determined 25. Diligent 26. Discerning 27. Disciplined 28. Encouraging 29. Enthusiastic 30. Fair 31. Faithful 32. Flexible 33. Forgiving 34. Friendly 35. Generous 36. Gentle 37. Giving 38. Godly 39. Graceful 40. Grateful 41. Happy 42. Helpful 43. Honest 44. Hospitable 45. Humble 46. Industrious 47. Ingenious 48. Insightful 49. Joyful 50. Kind 51. Loving 52. Loyal 53. Mature 54. Meek 55. Merciful 56. Modest 57. Moral 58. Neat 59. Observant 60. Optimistic 61. Organized 62. Patient 63. Peaceful 64. Persistent 65. Playful 66. Polite 67. Positive 68. Principled 69. Punctual 70. Reassuring 71. Relaxed 72. Reliable 73. Reflective 74. Respectful 75. Responsible 76. Reverent 77. Satisfied 78. Secure 79. Self-Controlled 80. Sensible 81. Sensitive 82. Sincere 83. Sociable 84. Steadfast 85. Straightforward 86. Supportive 87. Sympathetic 88. Tactful 89. Teachable 90. Tender 91. Thorough 92. Thoughtful 93. Trustworthy 94. Truthful 95. Understanding 96. Unselfish 97. Virtuous 98. Well-Mannered 99. Willing 100. Wise

ALICE GRAY, DR. STEVE STEPHENS, AND JOHN VAN DIEST

YOU CAN DO IT

You've got a telephone.
MAKE A CALL.

You've got paper.
WRITE A LETTER.

You've got a kitchen.
MAKE A MEAL.

You've got a billfold.
GIVE SOME MONEY.

You've got two hands.
PUT THEM TO WORK FOR OTHERS.

You've got two feet.
GO SEE A FRIEND IN PAIN.

You've got two ears.
LISTEN TO THE CRIES OF THE WOUNDED.

You've got two eyes.
LIFT THEM UP TO SEE THE WORLD AS GOD SEES IT.

You've got two lips.
PREACH THE GOSPEL OF PEACE.

RAV PRITCHARD
FROM "THE ABCS OF WISDOM"

TIMELESS GIFTS

TO YOUR NEIGHBORS—give thoughtful consideration. Be slow to gossip, quick to sympathize, ready to help—praying all the while that God will give them the necessary patience to live next to you.

TO EVERYONE YOU MEET—remember that each person carries burdens known only to himself or herself, and some have burdens too big to cope with—say the kind things you want (but hesitate) to say.

TO YOUR PARENTS—give loving appreciation for the years of time and effort—and money—that they invested in you. Do for them the little things that give them pleasure.

TO YOUR SPOUSE—remember how much he or she has had to put up with and for how long—give a frank, honest reappraisal of yourself. Ask yourself, "If I were my spouse, am I the sort of person I would want to come home to?"

TO YOUR CHILDREN—be more articulate about your appreciation of them as persons. You are not a perfect parent, but at least give them more of the one they do have—and make that one more loving. Be available, knowing that a parent needs to be, as God is, "a very present help in trouble." Take time to listen, time to play, time to counsel, time to encourage.

RUTH BELL GRAHAM
FROM "DECISION" MAGAZINE

CHOOSING HUMILITY IN AN ARROGANT WORLD

The humble can wait patiently,
while the arrogant wants it now!

The humble demonstrates kindness,
while the arrogant doesn't even notice the need.

The humble are content, not jealous or envious,
while the arrogant feel they deserve more.

The humble honors and esteems the other,
while the arrogant brags on himself.

The humble does not act unbecomingly,
while the arrogant's manners are rude.

The humble shows a servant spirit,
while the arrogant demands to be served.

The humble are not easily provoked,
while the arrogant are quick to take offense.

The humble quickly forgive a wrong suffered,
while the arrogant can't rest until they even the score.

H. DALE BURKE AND JAC LA TOUR
FROM "A LOVE THAT NEVER FAILS"

BASIC MANNERS THAT TEACH RESPECT

DO *make eye contact with people.*

DO *shake hands when you are introduced to new acquaintances.*

DON'T *interrupt when others are speaking.*

DO *open doors for others, particularly for women, elders, and superiors.*

DON'T *sit when others are standing.*

DO *address people as "Mr." "Mrs." or "Miss" until they give you permission to use a more familiar form of address.*

DON'T *call people by their last names only.*

DO *express an interest in other people.*

DON'T *refer to a person by derogatory names or ethnic terms.*

DO *ask others for their opinions.*

DON'T *confuse attacks on a person's character or intelligence with respectful disagreement.*

DO *praise publicly and reprimand privately.*

BOB HOSTETLER
FROM "HOMELIFE" MAGAZINE

WHY I WRITE THANK-YOU NOTES

1.

To acknowledge receipt of a gift

2.

To be courteous

3.

To express appreciation

4.

To reflect on the giver's thoughtfulness

5.

To absorb the blessing of being remembered

6.

To value their time and expense

7.

To seal it to my memory

8.

To encourage the giver

MARILYN MCAULEY
A WOMAN KNOWN FOR GRACIOUSNESS

VIRTUE

THE SECRET LIST OF
SOCIAL FAUX PAS

- Pointing

- Chewing gum in public

- Drinking loudly with a straw

- Breaking in line

- Loud music

- Talking during a church service

- Gossip

- Racial or ethnic jokes

- Poor hygiene

- Arguing in public

- Telling people off

- Leaving a party too soon

- Leaving a party too late

- Being disrespectful

- Interrupting others

- Being negative

- Reaching for food

- Leaning back in your chair

- Putting on airs

- Staring

- Shouting

- Not holding the door open for the next person

- Not giving up your seat to an older person

- Asking too many personal questions

- Confronting people to tell them it's your turn

ANN PLATZ AND SUSAN WALES
FROM "SOCIAL GRACES: MANNERS, CONVERSATION, AND CHARM FOR TODAY"

VIRTUE

A VIRTUOUS PERSON...

Is clean both inside and outside.

Neither looks up to the rich or down on the poor.

Loses, if need be, without squealing.

Wins without bragging.

Is always considerate of women, children, and old people.

Is too brave to lie.

Is too generous to cheat.

Takes his share of the world and lets other people have theirs.

GEORGE WASHINGTON CARVER
SCIENTIST AND INVENTOR

THREE BASIC INGREDIENTS
OF INTEGRITY

1.

Telling the truth.

2.

Keeping one's promises.

3.

Taking responsibility for one's behavior.

DR. ROSS CAMPBELL
FROM "RELATIONAL PARENTING"

GEORGE WASHINGTON'S
RULES OF CIVILITY

1. Every action done in company ought to be with some sign of respect to those that are present.

2. Show nothing to your friend that may frighten him.

3. In the presence of others sing not to yourself with a humming noise, nor drum with your fingers or feet.

4. Sleep not when others speak, sit not when others stand, speak not when you should hold your peace, walk not on when others stop.

5. Let your countenance be pleasant but in serious matters somewhat grave.

6. Show not yourself glad at the misfortune of another though he were your enemy.

7. Use no reproachful language against anyone, neither curse nor revile.

8. Associate yourself with men of good quality if you esteem your own reputation; for 'tis better to be alone than in bad company.

9. Speak not injurious words neither in jest nor earnest at none although they give occasion.

10. Think before you speak, pronounce not imperfectly nor bring out your words too hastily but orderly and distinctly.

11. Undertake not what you cannot perform but be careful to keep your promise.

12. Speak not evil of the absent for it is unjust.

13. When you speak of God or his attributes, let it be seriously and with reverence.

14. Labor to keep alive in your breast that little spark of celestial fire called conscience.

GEORGE WASHINGTON
FIRST PRESIDENT OF THE UNITED STATES

34 THINGS WE MUST RESPECT

1. God
2. Truth and wisdom
3. Life
4. Nature and all of creation
5. Our country
6. Our laws
7. Those older
8. Those younger
9. Our parents and grandparents
10. Our children
11. Our spouse
12. Our friends and neighbors
13. Those who teach us
14. Those who love us
15. Those who protect us
16. Those in charge of us
17. Those who look up to us
18. What does not belong to us
19. Compassion
20. Courage
21. Character
22. Humility
23. Peace
24. Patience and perseverance
25. Purity
26. Faith
27. Generosity
28. A task well done
29. A course well run
30. A life well lived
31. Our bodies
32. Our talents and abilities
33. Our mortality
34. All that is good and right and worthy of praise

DR. STEVE STEPHENS
PSYCHOLOGIST AND SEMINAR SPEAKER

SEVEN SACRED VIRTUES

Having HUMILITY instead of Pride
The humility to know that we are not alone in the world.

Having GENEROSITY instead of Covetousness
The generosity to allow others to have what they deserve.

Having RESTRAINT instead of Lust
The restraint to control our most passionate impulses.

Having KINDNESS instead of Anger
The kindness to tolerate the mistakes of our fellow man.

Having MODERATION instead of Gluttony
The moderation to satisfy ourselves with the necessities.

Having CHARITY instead of Envy
The charity to help those who are unable to help themselves.

Having DILIGENCE instead of Sloth
The diligence to make ourselves useful in the modern world.

MARILYN VOS SAVANT
FROM "PARADE" MAGAZINE

SCOUT'S LAW

A SCOUT IS...

TRUSTWORTHY.
A Scout tells the truth. He is honest,
and he keeps his promises. People can depend on him.

LOYAL.
A Scout is true to his family, friends, school, and nation.

HELPFUL.
A Scout cares about other people. He willingly volunteers
to help others without expecting payment or reward.

FRIENDLY.
A Scout is a friend to all.

COURTEOUS.
A Scout is polite to everyone regardless of age or
position. He knows that using good manners
makes it easier for people to get along.

KIND.
A Scout knows there is strength in being gentle.
He treats others as he wants to be treated.

OBEDIENT.

A Scout follows the rules of his family and school and obeys the laws of his community and country.

CHEERFUL.

A Scout looks for the bright side of life. He cheerfully does tasks that come his way. He tries to make others happy.

THRIFTY.

A Scout works to pay his way and to help others. He saves for the future.

BRAVE.

A Scout can face danger although he is afraid. He has the courage to stand for what he thinks is right even if others laugh at him or threaten him.

CLEAN.

A Scout keeps his body and mind fit. He chooses the company of those who live by high standards. He helps keep his home and community clean.

BOY SCOUTS OF AMERICA
NATIONAL COUNCIL

FRIENDSHIP

A heart for others

4

WHY FRIENDS ARE IMPORTANT

1.

They laugh with us.

2.

They cry with us.

3.

They build memories with us.

4.

They stand beside us.

5.

They confront us.

6.

They believe the best in us.

7.

They help us grow.

8.

They keep us from temptation.

9.

They enrich our lives.

DR. STEVE STEPHENS
PSYCHOLOGIST AND SEMINAR SPEAKER

10 RULES FOR GETTING
ALONG WITH PEOPLE

1.

Remember their names.

2.

Be comfortable to be with.
Don't cause strain in others.

3.

Try not to let things bother you.
Be easygoing.

4.

Don't be egotistical or know-it-all.

5.

Learn to be interesting so that people will
get something stimulating from being with you.

6.

Eliminate the "scratchy" elements in your personality,
traits that can irritate others.

7.

Never miss a chance to offer support
or say "Congratulations."

8.

Work at liking people.
Eventually you'll like them naturally.

9.

Honestly try to heal any misunderstandings
and drain off grievances.

10.

Develop spiritual depth in yourself
and share this strength with others.

NORMAN VINCENT PEALE
FROM "TIME TALK"

FRIENDSHIP

A FRIEND IS ONE WHO...

...follows through with what he or she says.

...understands and inspires.

...sacrifices for the other.

...invests in another.

...joyfully gives and serves.

...respects and honors.

...is courteous.

...builds character.

...loves at all times.

...challenges growth and maturity.

...tells the truth and restores dignity.

...keeps a promise.

...shares dreams.

...keeps in touch forever.

...is forgiving.

GLENDA HOTTON, M.A.
COUNSELOR

FRIENDSHIP WORDS

Concern

Courtesy

Contact

Caring

Comfort

Celebration

Cultivation

Connection

Continuity

Cherish

Companionship

Communication

Closeness

Consistency

EMILIE BARNES AND DONNA OTTO
FROM "FRIENDS OF THE HEART"

THE FOUR PROMISES
OF FORGIVENESS

1.

"I will no longer dwell on this incident."

2.

"I will not bring up this incident
again and use it against you."

3.

"I will not talk to others about this incident."

4.

"I will not allow this incident to stand
between us or hinder our relationship."

KEN SANDE
FROM "THE PEACEMAKER"

THE FINE ART OF FRIENDSHIP

1.
Develop friendships in which you demand nothing in return.

2.
Nurture an authentic interest in others.

3.
Always take time—often a long time—
to understand one another.

4.
Commit yourself to learning how to listen.

5.
Simply be there to care, whether you
know exactly what to do or not.

6.
Always treat others as equals.

7.
Be generous with legitimate praise and encouragement.

8.
Make your friends Number One,
preferring them above yourself.

9.
Emphasize the strengths and virtues of others,
not their sins and weaknesses.

DR. TED ENGSTROM
EXCERPTS FROM "CHRISTIAN LEADERSHIP LETTER"

20 QUESTIONS
TO ASK A FRIEND

These questions provide a fun forum for getting to know your new friends and for getting to know your old friends better. Use them for party games, for conversation starters. With an old and treasured friend, see how many you can guess about him or her.

1. Where did your family live when you were six? When you were twelve?

2. What was your favorite subject in school?

3. Have you ever played a musical instrument? What was it?

4. What is your favorite sport? Did you ever play it—or did you prefer to watch?

5. What was your least favorite food as a child?

6. Name your first boyfriend/girlfriend. How old were you when you met?

7. If you were beginning life again and could choose any career, what would you choose?

8. What is the most valuable thing you've learned in the past ten years?

9. What lost person or thing in your life do you miss the most?

10. What is the most encouraging word anyone can say to you?

11. Describe the most wonderful vacation you've ever taken. Why was it so great?

12. In what areas of your life do you feel most successful? Least successful?

13. What was the loneliest moment of your life? Why?

14. What single accomplishment in your life have you been proudest of?

15. What is your favorite season of the year and why?

16. Name an older person (not your parents) who influenced you as a younger person. What did you learn from that person?

17. If you had an unlimited budget to remodel just one room in your house, what would you do? In which room?

18. What was your favorite song when you were sixteen?

19. If you had to spend a year alone on a desert island and could take just three things with you, what would you take?

20. What's your idea of a truly perfect morning? What would you do?

EMILIE BARNES AND DONNA OTTO
FROM "FRIENDS OF THE HEART"

GOOD FRIENDS ARE HARD TO FIND

When things go sour and you really feel lousy,
do you have a friend you can tell?

Do you have a friend you can express any honest
thought to without fear of appearing foolish?

Do you have a friend who will let you
talk through a problem without giving you advice?
Who will just be a "sounding board"?

Will your friend risk your disapproval to suggest
you may be getting off track in your priorities?

Do you have a friend who will take the risk to
tell you that you are sinning? Or using poor judgment?

*

If you had a moral failure, do you know
that your friend would stand with you?

*

Is there a friend with whom you feel
you are facing life together?

*

Do you have a friend you believe you can trust, so if you
share confidential thoughts they will stay confidential?

*

When you are vulnerable and transparent with your friend,
are you convinced he or she will not think less of you?

*

Do you meet with a friend weekly or biweekly for
fellowship and prayer, and possibly for accountability?

PATRICK M. MORLEY
CONDENSED FROM "THE MAN IN THE MIRROR"

HEALTHY EXPECTATIONS
OF FRIENDS

Be honest.

Keep promises made.

Share ideas and dreams.

Have respect for my faith.

Never knowingly hurt me.

Purpose to resolve conflict.

Show respect for our differences.

Encourage my growth and maturity.

Demonstrate congruent values and beliefs.

GLENDA HOTTON, M.A.
COUNSELOR

UNHEALTHY EXPECTATIONS
OF FRIENDS

Never disagree with my ideas.

Have no other friends but me.

Love my family and friends.

Call or see me every day.

Do whatever I request.

Like everything I like.

Be perfect.

GLENDA HOTTON, M.A.
COUNSELOR

ANTIGOSSIP PACT

In 1752, a group of Methodist men, including John Wesley, signed a covenant that each man agreed to hang on the wall of his study. The six articles of this solemn agreement were as follows:

1. That we will not listen or willingly inquire after ill concerning one another;

2. That, if we do hear any ill of each other, we will not be forward to believe it;

3. That as soon as possible we will communicate what we hear by speaking or writing to the person concerned;

4. That until we have done this, we will not write or speak a syllable of it to any other person;

5. That neither will we mention it, after we have done this, to any other person;

6. That we will not make any exception to any of these rules unless we think ourselves absolutely obliged in conference.

JOHN WESLEY AND FRIENDS
FROM "GOD'S LITTLE DEVOTIONAL BOOK"

PROVERBS ON FRIENDSHIP

A true friend is always loyal, and
a brother is born to help in time of need.
PROVERBS 17:17

Wounds from a friend are better than kisses from an enemy!
PROVERBS 27:6

There are "friends" who pretend to be friends,
but there is a friend who sticks closer than a brother.
PROVERBS 18:24

Love forgets mistakes; nagging about
them parts the best of friends.
PROVERBS 17:9

Never abandon a friend—either yours or your father's.
Then you won't need to go to a distant
relative for help in your time of need.
PROVERBS 27:10

KING SOLOMON
THE BOOK OF PROVERBS

GREAT SAYINGS ON FRIENDSHIP

❧

A friend is a present you give yourself.
ROBERT LOUIS STEVENSON

❧

A friend is one who makes me do my best.
OSWALD CHAMBERS

❧

The only way to have a friend is to be one.
RALPH WALDO EMERSON

❧

Give and take makes good friends.
SCOTTISH SAYING

❧

Loyalty is what we seek in friendship.
CICERO

❧

To have a good friend is one of the highest delights of life;
to be a good friend is one of the noblest
and most difficult undertakings.
AUTHOR UNKNOWN

❧

The real friend is he or she who can share all
our sorrow and double our joys.
B. C. FORBES

A cheerful friend is like a sunny day,
which sheds its brightness on all around.
JOHN LUBBOCK

One who knows how to show and to accept kindness
will be a friend better than any possession.
SOPHOCLES

In prosperity our friends know us;
in adversity we know our friends.
JOHN CHURTON COLLINS

Friendship begins with gratitude.
GERTRUDE ELIOT

If you want an accounting of your worth,
count your friends.
MERRY BROWNE

10 IDEAS FOR STAYING CLOSE
WHEN YOU'RE FAR AWAY

1. ORGANIZE A REUNION.
How often you do this will depend on time, distance,
finances, and many other factors. But if at all possible,
try to get together in person at least once a year.

2. INVEST IN MA BELL.
The telephone can be a lifeline between long-distance friends.
Think of the bills as investments in your friendship.

3. DON'T FORGET TO WRITE.
There's just something special about receiving a card
or letter in the mailbox. A letter, unlike a phone call,
can be reread and treasured for years.

4. GO HIGH TECH.
If you have a computer or fax, explore the advantages
of using these high-tech tools to keep in touch.
E-mail is an especially handy, immediate, and inexpensive
way to keep current with long-distance friends.

5. SEND PICTURES.
This is a great way to keep current with each other's lives.
Do you have duplicate shots of the same pose?
Send one to your friend with a note on the back.

6. VACATION TOGETHER.

Meet somewhere between your homes for a week of
fun and renewing your friendship. Check out
hotels, resorts, spas, or retreat centers.

7. WORK TOGETHER ON A LONG-DISTANCE PROJECT.

Planning a college reunion or cosponsoring a child from another
country gives you an excuse and a reminder to stay in touch.

8. AT LEAST SAY HI.

During very busy times when you barely have time to breathe,
much less write or even phone, a simple postcard or a five-minute
phone call can still keep the lines of communication open.

9. PRAY FOR EACH OTHER

—always and faithfully.

10. SEND YOUR FRIEND A SUBSCRIPTION OR ENROLL HIM OR HER IN AN "OF THE MONTH" CLUB.

Whether it's magazines, books, flowers, fruits, or even steaks,
the monthly arrival will bring thoughts of you. Just be sure the
subscription doesn't require your friend to do or pay something!

EMILIE BARNES AND DONNA OTTO
CONDENSED FROM "FRIENDS OF THE HEART"

10 COMMANDMENTS OF FRIENDSHIP

1. SPEAK TO PEOPLE.

There is nothing as nice as a cheerful word of greeting.

2. SMILE AT PEOPLE.

It takes 72 muscles to frown, but only 14 to smile!

3. CALL PEOPLE BY NAME.

The sweetest music to anyone's ear

is the sound of his or her own name.

4. BE FRIENDLY AND HELPFUL.

If you would have friends, be friendly.

5. BE CORDIAL.

Speak and act as if everything you do were a real pleasure.

6. BE GENUINELY INTERESTED IN PEOPLE.

You can like everyone IF YOU TRY.

7. BE GENEROUS WITH PRAISE, CAUTIOUS WITH CRITICISM.

Try for a ratio of seven praises to each criticism.

8. BE CONSIDERATE OF THE FEELINGS OF OTHERS.

It will be appreciated.

9. BE THOUGHTFUL OF THE OPINIONS OF OTHERS.

People love their opinions as they do their own children;

calling them ugly won't get you anything but anger.

10. BE ALERT TO GIVE SERVICE.

What counts most in life is what we do for others!

AUTHOR UNKNOWN
FROM "THE POWER OF ENCOURAGEMENT"

FRIENDSHIP

FUN ACTIVITIES FOR COUPLE FRIENDS

Take a trip to the mountains.

Plan a picnic in the park.

Cook dinner together.

Visit a museum.

Go hiking.

Start a book club.

Share prayer requests.

Learn a new card game together.

Rent old movies.

Fly kites.

Attend a play or sporting event.

Explore an arts and crafts fair.

Rest and relax at a recreation area such as a lake, river, or park.

TRICIA GOVER
CONDENSED FROM "HOMELIFE" MAGAZINE

BEING A GOOD NEIGHBOR

Share your time and your possessions.

Be friendly, but respect their space.

Watch what you say over the fence.

Be a good listener.

Respect sleeping hours (between 10 P.M. and 8 A.M.).

Be positive and cheerful.

Provide meals when there is an illness, birth, death, or crisis.

Watch their property when they aren't home.

Volunteer to pick up mail, water plants, or feed pets when they are away.

Help out when they are working on a big project.

Remember them at Christmas.

Treat them as you'd like to be treated.

TAMI STEPHENS
MOTHER OF THREE

HEALTH

A long and satisfying life

5

STRESS BUSTERS

Take a break.

Take a bath.

Take a walk.

Take a breath.

Take a nap.

ALICE GRAY, DR. STEVE STEPHENS, AND JOHN VAN DIEST

GUIDELINES FOR GOOD SLEEP

- § Get up about the same time every day.

- § Go to bed only when you are sleepy.

- § Establish relaxing presleep rituals such as a warm bath, a light bedtime snack, or ten minutes of reading.

- § Exercise regularly. If you exercise vigorously, do this at least six hours before bedtime. Mild exercise—such as simple stretching or walking—should not be done within four hours of bedtime.

- § Maintain a regular schedule. Regular times for meals, taking medications, doing chores, and other activities help keep your "inner clock" running smoothly.

- § Don't eat or drink anything containing caffeine within six hours of bedtime. Don't drink alcohol within several hours of bedtime, or when you are sleepy. Tiredness can intensify the effects of alcohol.

- § Avoid smoking close to bedtime.

- § If you take naps, try to do so at the same time every day. For most people, a midafternoon nap is most helpful.

- § Avoid sleeping pills, or use them conservatively. Most doctors avoid prescribing sleeping pills for a duration of longer than three weeks. Never drink alcohol while taking sleeping pills.

AMERICAN ACADEMY OF SLEEP MEDICINE

HOW TO KEEP YOUR
IMMUNE SYSTEM STRONG

Practice good nutrition.

Stop smoking.

Get regular exercise.

Avoid physical stress.

Avoid emotional stress.

Watch your weight.

Stop environmental pollution.

Keep a positive attitude.

Pray as often as possible.

TERRY T. SHINTANI, M.D., M.P.H
DIRECTOR OF INTEGRATIVE MEDICINE, WAIMAE COAST HEALTH CENTER

20 WAYS TO RELAX

1.
Watch a sunrise.

2.
Learn to play a musical instrument.

3.
Sing in the shower.

4.
Never refuse homemade brownies.

5.
Whistle.

6.
Take someone bowling.

7.
Sing in a choir.

8.
Be romantic.

9.
Buy a bird feeder and place it where
it can be seen from your kitchen window.

10.
Wave at children on school buses.

11.
Lie on your back and look at the stars.

12.
Rekindle old friendships.

13.
Reread your favorite book.

14.
Try everything offered by
supermarket food demonstrators.

15.
Never waste an opportunity to
tell someone you love them.

16.
Save one evening a week
for just you and your spouse.

17.
Begin each day with your favorite music.

18.
Laugh a lot.

19.
Give thanks for every meal.

20.
Count your blessings.

H. JACKSON BROWN, JR.
CONDENSED FROM "LIFE'S LITTLE INSTRUCTION BOOK"

HEALTH

WHY LAUGHTER IS HEALTHY

It is contagious.

> *When you laugh, so do others.*

It kills depression.

> *It is hard to laugh and be depressed simultaneously.*

It reduces stress.

> *By distracting you from the worries and seriousness of life.*

It attracts others.

> *People are drawn to a warm smile and a hearty laugh.*

It makes difficult situations tolerable.

> *A laugh lightens even the heaviest load.*

DR. STEVE STEPHENS
PSYCHOLOGIST AND SEMINAR SPEAKER

FIVE TIPS FOR STAYING YOUNG

1.

Your mind is not old; keep developing it.

2.

Your humor is not over; keep enjoying it.

3.

Your strength is not gone; keep using it.

4.

Your opportunities have not vanished; keep pursuing them.

5.

God is not dead; keep seeking Him.

AUTHOR UNKNOWN

WARNING SIGNS OF EMOTIONAL PAIN

- ☙ Do you live in your past and worry about your future?

- ☙ Are you depressed and feeling empty inside?

- ☙ Do you feel defeated because of a poor self-image?

- ☙ Are you in bondage to other people's opinions of you?

- ☙ Do you take everyone's stress personally or fall apart when someone looks at you the wrong way?

- ☙ Do you keep yourself excessively busy to the point that your life feels out of control?

- ☙ Do you have compulsive behavior patterns?

- ☙ Do you feel guilty for saying no, even if you've said it for the right reasons?

- ☙ Are you paralyzed by fear?

- ☙ Do you have a short fuse? How do you react to disappointment?

- ☙ Do you have a history of destructive relationships?

- ☙ Are you an approval addict?

SHERI ROSE SHEPHERD
FROM "FIT FOR EXCELLENCE"

DON'TS FOR EMOTIONAL FITNESS

❦ DON'T IGNORE IT!

Ignoring the warning signs will not make them go away any more than ignoring a gas tank that says "empty" will allow the car to continue to run.

❦ DON'T EXCUSE IT!

Many of us make excuses for our emotional pain rather then looking at the problem that's causing it.

❦ DON'T DECORATE IT!

Many times we decorate our pain with a pretty house, pretty clothes, and prestigious positions.

❦ DON'T COVER IT UP!

Many of us cover up with accomplishments and excessive busyness.

❦ DON'T PRETEND IT'S NOT THERE!

Many of us have no idea why we're feeling pain because we pretend that everything is okay.

❦ DON'T POSTPONE DEALING WITH IT!

Don't postpone dealing with your warning signs, or they will deal with you.

SHERI ROSE SHEPHERD
FROM "FIT FOR EXCELLENCE"

RESULTS OF ANXIETY

DIVIDES OUR MINDS

Instead of focusing on goals, the stress-filled person allows anxiety to steal many of his thoughts.

DRAINS OUR ENERGY

Naturally, when we are consumed with a situation, the psychological and emotional calisthenics sap strength. Anxiety slows productivity. Reduced energy means poor production and poor judgment.

AFFECTS RELATIONSHIPS

Friends and family also suffer when we allow the drone of worry's whispers to keep us in the dumps.

CAUSES US TO MAKE UNWISE DECISIONS

Mistakes come when we try in our own strength and timing to remedy a situation that God will handle if we only wait in faith.

STEALS OUR PEACE AND JOY

This is evidence that stress and worry are tools of the enemy. Peace and joy are gifts from God, regardless of the storm.

HARMS OUR PHYSICAL BODIES

Our bodies deteriorate under the weight we try to carry on our shoulders.

CHARLES STANLEY
FROM IN "IN TOUCH" MAGAZINE

AVOID GETTING AND DOING TOO MUCH

- Is this really important to me?

- Do I truly enjoy this?

- Do I really need this?

- Does this cause stress and drain my energy?

- Does this cause me to hurry too much?

- What are healthier alternatives?

- How did I manage without this?

ROBERT AND DEBRA BRUCE AND ELLEN OLDACRE
FROM "STANDING UP AGAINST THE ODDS"

HEALTH

WHAT GUYS NEED TO KNOW ABOUT PMS

1.
It's Real.

2.
Respect Her Feelings.

3.
Don't Take It Personally.

4.
Get Educated.

5.
Help Her Understand Her Options.

6.
Don't Try to Fix Her.

7.
Pray for Her and with Her.

8.
Learn to Communicate.

J. RON EAKER, M.D.
CONDENSED FROM "NEW MAN" MAGAZINE

DEFUSING ANGER

1.
KEEP SHORT ACCOUNTS.
This serves to minimize the pent-up
emotions that lead to anger.

2.
THINK BEFORE YOU SPEAK.
If you dump the whole emotional load first,
without thinking, you'll spend more time
than you care to imagine cleaning up the mess.

3.
DESCRIBE HOW YOU FEEL.
Preferably in a controlled tone of voice;
you're likely to create a cooler atmosphere.

4.
SEEK RESOLUTION QUICKLY.
Anger left to fester becomes a deep emotional
infection that only gets worse as time passes.

H. DALE BURKE AND JAC LA TOUR
CONDENSED FROM "A LOVE THAT NEVER FAILS"

TOP 10 HABITS FOR
HEALTH AND VITALITY

1. GO TO SLEEP.

Most of us need at least eight hours of slumber and we're not getting it. If you rearrange your night and morning routines to provide the sleep you need, you (and your coworkers) will notice a positive difference!

2. GIVE YOURSELF A BREAK.

Midmorning and midafternoon, retreat from your work station for ten minutes and shift your mind into neutral. Do some deep breathing and stretch to loosen neck, shoulder, and back muscles. Take a brief walk or climb and descend a stairwell. After just a few minutes you will feel calm and refreshed.

3. ENJOY THESE HEALTHY FOODS AS OFTEN AS YOU CAN.

These foods are especially effective in supplying your body and brain with the nutrients they need for strength and efficiency—while helping prevent problems such as cancer, heart attack, diabetes, and stroke: fresh, brightly colored fruits and vegetables, whole grains, olive oil, nuts (especially walnuts), salmon and tuna, and green and black tea.

4. SAY GOOD-BYE TO AN UNHEALTHY HABIT.

Do you smoke? Over-imbibe alcohol, coffee, soft drinks, high-fat foods or snacks? Pick one unhealthy habit you'd like to stop—just one for now—and dedicate yourself to expunging it from your life. Then, one at a time, knock off your other unhealthy habits.

5. LAUGH!

Laughter releases powerful endorphins that soothe your nerves and strengthen mind, body, and spirit against the stresses of life. Look for the lighter side (it's there!) and let 'er rip.

6. SUPPLEMENT YOUR NUTRITION

As we grow older we should pay special attention to our intake of calcium for bone density and to selenium and vitamins C, E, and beta carotene for their antioxidant benefits.

7. GET AWAY FROM IT ALL—SOON AND OFTEN.

Spread out your vacations and long weekends to provide frequent getaways from your everyday labors. There's a huge, wonderful world outside your window—take full advantage of it.

8. GET MOVING.

A brisk thirty-minute walk, jog, bike ride, or aerobic workout at least three days a week for the cardiovascular system. A moderate resistance workout three days each week for muscle tone and strength. Aerobic and resistance training are not only essential for health and vitality, but they also work wonders for morale!

9. MAKE WATER YOUR BEVERAGE OF CHOICE.

Water flushes toxins from your system and supplies your cells with the life-giving elements they need. Drink at least *eight* glasses each day. More before, during, and after exercise.

10. COVER UP.

With skin cancers on the rise, there is no such thing as a healthy suntan. If you spend time outside during the day, do yourself and your loved ones a big favor: Cover as much skin as possible. What you can't cover, use a sunscreen.

DAN BENSON
FROM "THE NEW RETIREMENT:
HOW TO SECURE FINANCIAL FREEDOM AND LIVE OUT YOUR DREAMS"

EATING HEALTHY

❧ Maintain a desirable weight.

❧ Restrict fat.

❧ Get enough fiber

   whole-grain cereals, breads, and pasta; vegetables; fruit.

❧ Eat foods rich in vitamin A

   yellow/orange fruits and yellow/orange or dark green vegetables.

❧ Eat foods rich in vitamin C

   citrus fruits, strawberries, tomatoes, raw or lightly-cooked green vegetables.

❧ Eat more cabbage-family vegetables

   cabbage, broccoli, brussels sprouts, cauliflower. Restrict salt-cured, smoked, and nitrite-cured foods.

❧ Avoid/restrict alcoholic beverages.

THE HOPE HEART INSTITUTE
CONDENSED FROM "LIFEWISE" NEWSLETTER

GUIDELINES FOR CHOOSING HEALTHY FOODS

1. CHOOSE A WIDE VARIETY OF FOODS.
No one food or small selection of foods will
meet all your nutritional needs.

2. SELECT A MAJORITY OF YOUR FOODS
FROM FRUITS, VEGETABLES, AND WHOLE GRAINS.
Eat at least five servings of fruits and vegetables and six to
eleven servings of whole grain foods each day.

3. CHOOSE LOW-FAT FOODS.
Keep your fat intake to 30 percent or less of your
daily total calorie intake.

4. EAT SMALLER PORTIONS OF MEATS.
Six to eight ounces per day is enough to
support your need for protein.

5. EAT CALCIUM-RICH FOODS EACH DAY.

6. EAT WHEN YOU ARE HUNGRY.
Stop when you are satisfied.

7. DRINK AT LEAST 64 OUNCES OF WATER EACH DAY.

BRANDA POLK
FROM "HOMELIFE" MAGAZINE

TRAVEL FIRST-AID KIT

- A thermometer
- An assortment of bandages, including gauze and tape
- Pain medication
- An antiseptic
- Cotton swabs and cotton balls
- A large clean handkerchief in case you need to make a temporary sling
- Insect repellent
- Sunscreen
- Cold medication
- Diarrhea medication
- Antacids

KATE REDD
FROM "52 WAYS TO MAKE FAMILY TRAVEL MORE ENJOYABLE"

STAY ACTIVE

Go for a ten-minute walk after each meal.

Walk or use your bike to run small errands.

Park your car in the space farthest from where you're going.

Get off the bus a stop or two early and walk the rest of the way.

Take the stairs instead of the elevator.

AMY GIVLER
FROM "HOMELIFE" MAGAZINE

HOW TO STOP SMOKING

THINK ABOUT WHY YOU SMOKE.

Are you trying to look more mature? Do you think smoking makes you less anxious? Do stressful situations trigger your smoking? Have you tried to quit but couldn't (and now you realize you're addicted)?

THINK ABOUT HOW SMOKING HURTS YOU.

It makes you smell bad and have bad breath. It's expensive. It interferes with your stamina and makes you more anxious, not less. Also, you're more likely to get sick or have allergies.

SET A QUIT DATE WITHIN THE NEXT TWO WEEKS.

Tell everyone you know. Throw away cigarettes and ashtrays. Plan to avoid situations that always lead to smoking (such as reading the newspaper with a cup of coffee after breakfast).

QUIT.

You may feel some withdrawal symptoms (crankiness, trouble sleeping, fuzzy-headedness), but they will pass. Chew sugar-free gum. Drink lots of water to flush the tobacco toxins from your system.

REWARD YOURSELF (BUT NOT WITH FOOD).

You've done it! You've become a nonsmoker.

AMY GIVLER
FROM "HOMELIFE" MAGAZINE

CONTENTMENT

Finding peace and fulfillment

6

SEVEN WONDERS OF THE WORLD

1.
Seeing

2.
Hearing

3.
Tasting

4.
Touching

5.
Running

6.
Laughing

7.
Loving

A LITTLE GIRL
(WRITTEN WHEN HER TEACHER ASKED THE CLASS TO MAKE
A LIST OF THE SEVEN NATURAL WONDERS OF THE WORLD)

CONTENTMENT

WHAT MONEY CAN
AND CANNOT BUY

A bed but not sleep.

Books but not brains.

Food but not appetite.

Finery but not beauty.

A house but not a home.

Medicine but not health.

Luxuries but not culture.

Amusements but not happiness.

Companions but not friends.

Flattery but not respect.

AUTHOR UNKNOWN

ONE IS POOR IF HE...

Cannot enjoy what he has.

Is not content.

Is short on good works.

Has no self-respect.

Has no real friends.

Has lost the zest for living.

Has little joy.

Has lost his health.

Has no eternal hope.

LEROY BROWNLOW
CONDENSED FROM "A PSALM IN MY HEART"

I AM THANKFUL FOR...

...the mess to clean after a party because it means I have been surrounded by friends.

...the taxes I pay because it means that I'm employed.

...the clothes that fit a little too snug because it means I have enough to eat.

...my shadow who watches me work because it means that I am out in the sunshine.

...a lawn that needs mowing, windows that need cleaning and gutters that need fixing because it means I have a home.

...the spot I find at the far end of the parking lot because it means I am capable of walking.

...all the complaining I hear about our government because it means we have freedom of speech.

...my huge heating bill because it means I am warm.

...the lady behind me in church who sings off key because it means that I can hear.

...the alarm that goes off in the early morning hours because it means that I'm alive.

...the piles of laundry and ironing because it means my loved ones are nearby.

...weariness and aching muscles at the end of the day because it means I have been productive.

NANCIE J. CARMODY
FROM "FAMILY CIRCLE" MAGAZINE

JOY FOR TODAY

I would like to read a noble poem.

I would like to see a beautiful picture.

I would like to hear a bit of inspiring music.

I would like to meet a great soul.

I would like to say a few sensible words.

GOETHE
PHILOSOPHER AND PLAYWRIGHT

IF I HAD IT TO DO OVER AGAIN

§ I would love my wife more in front of my children.

§ I would laugh with my children more—at our mistakes and joys.

§ I would listen more—even to the youngest child.

§ I would be more honest about my own weaknesses and stop pretending perfection.

§ I would do more things with my children.

§ I would be more encouraging and bestow more praise.

§ I would pay more attention to little things, deeds, and words of love and kindness.

JOHN MACARTHUR
FROM "THE FAMILY"

CONTENTMENT

RANDOM ACTS OF KINDNESS

1. Let someone cut in front of you. 2. Send a thank-you note. 3. Take a bag of groceries to someone in need. 4. Volunteer. 5. Give a larger tip than normal. 6. Open a door for someone. 7. Visit the elderly. 8. Pick up letters. 9. Write a note of encouragement to a teenager. 10. Invite a widow to dinner. 11. Be polite. 12. Take a neighbor flowers. 14. Bake something for a friend. 15. Listen. 16. Watch someone's children. 17. Ask, "What can I do for you?" 18. Invite someone new for coffee. 19. Make a new employee feel welcome. 20. Smile at a stranger. 21. Be a Big Brother or Big Sister. 22. Help without being asked. 23. Compliment five people each day. 24. Offer to pick up a neighbor's mail. 25. Talk respectfully. 26. Donate to a nonprofit organization. 27. Send a gift anonymously. 28. Visit someone in the hospital. 29. Feed the birds. 30. Do for others what you would like them to do for you.

ALICE GRAY, DR. STEVE STEPHENS, AND JOHN VAN DIEST

TRANQUILITY

⚘ You can have peace in your heart with little if you are in the will of God; but you can be miserable with much if you are out of His will.

⚘ You can have joy in obscurity if you are in the will of God, but you can be wretched with wealth and fame out of His will.

⚘ You can be happy in the midst of sufferings if you are in God's will, but you can have agony in good health out of His will.

⚘ You can be contented in poverty if you are in the will of God, but you can be wretched in riches out of His will.

⚘ You can be calm and at peace in the midst of persecution as long as you are in the will of God, but you can be miserable and defeated in the midst of acclaim if you are out of His will.

BILLY GRAHAM
FROM "UNTO THE HILLS"

CONTENTMENT

RULES OF CONTENTMENT

Allow ourselves to complain of nothing, not even the weather.

Never picture ourselves in any circumstances in which we are not.

Never compare our lot with that of another.

Never allow ourselves to wish that this or that had been otherwise.

Never dwell on the tomorrow; remember, that is God's and not ours.

E. B. PUSEY
ENGLISH THEOLOGIAN

WE ALL NEED...

TO BE LOVED ...*when lonely.*

TO BE PROTECTED ...*when afraid.*

TO BE COMFORTED ...*when hurting.*

TO BE FED ...*when hungry.*

TO BE TAUGHT ...*when confused.*

TO BE ENCOURAGED ...*when downhearted.*

TO BE FILLED ...*when empty.*

TO BE HEARD ...*when crying.*

TO BE FOUND ...*when lost.*

TO BE GIVEN HOPE ...*when all seems dark.*

DR. STEVE STEPHENS
PSYCHOLOGIST AND SEMINAR SPEAKER

CONTENTMENT

20 WAYS TO SIMPLIFY

1. Eliminate ten things from your life.

2. Cut back on TV.

3. Escape to a quiet spot.

4. Set your own pace.

5. Get rid of clutter.

6. When you bring in something new, throw out something old.

7. Do only one thing at a time.

8. Say no at least once a day.

9. Enjoy the little things.

10. Take at least four breaks per day.

11. Determine what really matters.

12. Make peace with all people.

13. Tell the truth.

14. Appreciate beauty.

15. If you don't need it, don't buy it.

16. If you don't have time, don't do it.

17. Have a place for everything and put everything in its place.

18. Share your thoughts, feelings, and opinions with a friend every day.

19. Allow time to pray.

20. Thank God for what you have.

DR. STEVE STEPHENS
PSYCHOLOGIST AND SEMINAR SPEAKER

CONTENTMENT

HAPPINESS

❦ Happiness comes from spiritual wealth,
not material wealth.

❦ Happiness comes from giving, not getting.

❦ If we try hard to bring happiness to others,
we cannot stop it from coming to us also.

❦ To get joy, we must give it.

❦ To keep joy, we must scatter it.

JOHN TEMPLETON
FROM "MORE OF...THE BEST OF BITS & PIECES"

LIFE IS HARD...BUT GOD IS GOOD

HE IS STRONG *in our weakness.*

HE IS COMFORT *when we're in pain.*

HE IS LOVE *when we need acceptance.*

HE IS PEACE *when we're haunted by fear.*

HE IS PROTECTION *when we're in trouble.*

HE HEALS OUR WOUNDS *when someone or something has hurt us.*

HE IS OUR JOY *when our hearts are grieved.*

HE IS OUR FRIEND *when we've been rejected.*

HE IS OUR POWER *when we need a miracle.*

SHERI ROSE SHEPHERD
FROM "FIT FOR EXCELLENCE"

THE GREATEST THINGS

The best day, today;

The best play, work;

The greatest puzzle, life;

The greatest thought, God;

The greatest mystery, death;

The best work, work you like;

The most ridiculous asset, pride;

The greatest need, common sense;

The most expensive indulgence, hate;

The most disagreeable person, the complainer;

The best teacher, the one who makes you want to learn;

The greatest deceiver, the one who deceives himself;

The worst bankrupt, the soul who has lost enthusiasm;

The cheapest, easiest, and most stupid thing to do, finding fault;

The greatest comfort, the knowledge that
you have done your work well;

The most agreeable companion, the one who
would not have you any different than you are;

The meanest feeling, being envious of another's success;

The greatest thing in the world, love—for family,
home, friends, neighbors.

AUTHOR UNKNOWN

CONTENTMENT

FOUR THINGS THAT
BRING GREAT PEACE

1.
Strive to do another's will rather than your own.

2.
Always prefer to have less than more.

3.
Always seek the lower place and be submissive in all things.

4.
Always wish and pray that God's will
may be entirely fulfilled in you.

THOMAS Á KEMPIS
FROM "THE IMITATION OF CHRIST"

THE POWER OF SILENCE

It makes room for LISTENING.

It gives us freedom to OBSERVE.

It allows time to THINK.

It provides space in which to FEEL.

It lets us broaden our AWARENESS.

It opens us to the entry of PEACE.

AUTHOR UNKNOWN

MARRIAGE AND ROMANCE

Experiencing the best

7

12 ACTIONS FOR
A HAPPY MARRIAGE

Ask

Listen

Accept

Respect

Risk

Encourage

Adjust

Forgive

Give

Love

Laugh

Comfort

DR. STEVE STEPHENS
PSYCHOLOGIST AND SEMINAR SPEAKER

THE FIVE LOVE LANGUAGES

1.
WORDS OF AFFIRMATION

Compliments, words of encouragement, and requests rather than demands all affirm the self-worth of your spouse.

2.
QUALITY TIME

Spending quality time together through sharing, listening, and participating in joint meaningful activities communicates that we truly care for and enjoy each other.

3.
GIFTS

Gifts are visual symbols of love, whether they are items you purchased or made, or are merely your own presence made available to your spouse. Gifts demonstrate that you care, and they represent the value of the relationship.

4.
ACTS OF SERVICE

Criticism of your spouse's failure to do things for you may be an indication that "acts of service" is your primary love language. Acts of service should never be coerced but should be freely given and received, and completed as requested.

5.
PHYSICAL TOUCH

Physical touch, as a gesture of love, reaches to the depths of our being. As a love language, it is a powerful form of communication—from the smallest touch on the shoulder to the most passionate kiss.

GARY CHAPMAN
FROM "THE FIVE LOVE LANGUAGES"

BETWEEN A HUSBAND AND WIFE

§ We provide emotional, physical, and spiritual safety.

§ We promise unconditional love and acceptance.

§ We say in a hundred ways, "We belong together, here!"

§ We provide for, and are sensitive to, each other's needs.

§ We're loyal to each other—against all rumor and criticism; in the face of failure; in spite of disappointments.

DAVID AND HEATHER KOPP
CONDENSED FROM "UNQUENCHABLE LOVE"

A REGRET-FREE MARRIAGE

1.

Refuse to divorce.

2.

Make your mate's happiness a priority.

3.

Avoid hurtful words with your mate.

4.

Build memories with your mate.

ROBERT JEFFRESS
FROM "SAY GOODBYE TO REGRET"

QUESTIONS TO ASK
BEFORE YOU SAY "I DO"

1.
How does he treat his parents?

2.
Can you accept her for who she is if she never changes?

3.
What sort of people does he spend his time with?

4.
Does she have any addictive tendencies?

5.
Is he trustworthy?

6.
What is her reputation?

7.
What do your family and friends think of him?

8.
What is her philosophy of life?

9.
What is his spiritual life like?

10.
Do you respect her?

11.
What are his strengths and weaknesses?

12.
What are her parents like?

13.
What is his track record with past relationships?

14.
Is she kindhearted?

15.
What does he expect of you?

16.
How does she handle money?

17.
How does he respond to stress?

18.
How does she spend her leisure time?

19.
What are his likes and dislikes?

20.
What are her plans and dreams for the future?

DR. STEVE STEPHENS
PSYCHOLOGIST AND SEMINAR SPEAKER

21 THINGS EVERY COUPLE SHOULD KNOW

1. The qualities within your spouse that ignited your interest when you first met.

2. How to give your spouse a visible expression of love.

3. The importance of looking into your spouse's eyes while listening.

4. One compliment a day isn't too many.

5. Good memories are priceless no matter what they cost.

6. The importance of courtship after marriage.

7. How to make your spouse laugh.

8. The simple intimacy of holding hands.

9. A romantic location within walking distance from your home.

10. Unexpected gifts can bring great pleasure.

11. Marriages are built on small expressions of affection.

12. How to appreciate and accept the differences in your partner.

13. How to say, "I'm sorry."

14. How to agree more and argue less.

15. Being the right person is more important than trying to change your spouse into the right person.

16. How to make every anniversary a special celebration.

17. A growing marriage gets stronger and better over the years.

18. Guidelines for a great marriage won't work unless you apply them.

19. The triggers that hurt feelings.

20. The value of a hug.

21. Your spouse is priceless.

DOUG FIELDS
SELECTED FROM "365 THINGS EVERY COUPLE SHOULD KNOW"

NINE WAYS TO
E-N-C-O-U-R-A-G-E EACH OTHER

Express love.

Nurture your relationship.

Cooperate with each other.

Observe ways to creatively demonstrate love.

Understand, don't lecture.

Remember your blessings.

Accept each other.

Grow together.

Enjoy each other.

DUANE STOREY AND SANFORD KULKIN
FROM "BODY AND SOUL"

50 FUN THINGS TO DO WITH YOUR SPOUSE

1. Look at picture albums. 2. Have a candlelight dinner. 3. Give each other fifteen-minute backrubs. 4. Make a date for a concert or a play. 5. Listen to your favorite recording. 6. Take a short walk. 7. Go window-shopping. 8. Tell each other two jokes. 9. Write a poem to each other. 10. Go to a movie. 11. Play charades. 12. Buy a plant. 13. Read a book, story, or article together. 14. Plan a trip to the zoo. 15. Sing some songs together. 16. Bake cookies together (clean up, too). 17. Make a surprise visit to someone. 18. Go bowling. 19. Make valentines for each other. 20. Read The Song of Solomon. 21. Play hide-and-seek. 22. Talk about favorite memories. 23. Go camping (campground or yard). 24. Go bicycle riding. 25. Have a wiener roast. 26. Call your spouse just to say "I love you." 27. Send flowers for no special reason. 28. Call and invite your spouse to lunch. 29. Put a love note where your spouse can find it. 30. Make popcorn or fudge. 31. Tell each other bedtime stories. 32. Go for a scenic drive. 33. Act out a play or skit with each other. 34. Plan a trip to the beach. 35. Spend a day in the city. 36. Surprise the other with dinner reservations. 37. Spend a night at a motel or hotel. 38. Play a favorite board game. 39. Spend an afternoon hiking. 40. Finger paint. 41. Go on a picnic. 42. Play racquetball or tennis. 43. Go out to breakfast. 44. Work in the yard together. 45. Wash the car together. 46. Have a pillow fight. 47. Make love by candlelight. 48. Take a class together. 49. Spend an evening in front of the fireplace. 50. Attend a sporting event.

DR. STEVE STEPHENS
PSYCHOLOGIST AND SEMINAR SPEAKER

THE TOP 10 MISTAKES COUPLES MAKE

1. AVOID CONFLICT.

Avoided conflict requires repression of anger, which leads to depression of feelings. A genuinely passionate partnership requires conflict, not terminal niceness or withdrawal.

2. AVOID EACH OTHER.

Occasional withdrawal is healthy. Habitual withdrawal (stonewalling) is death to partnership.

3. ESCALATE.

Conflict, skillfully handled, is one of the keys to a great relationship. Conflict out of control is an excuse for physical, verbal, or psychological abuse.

4. CRITICIZE.

Habitually speaking (or thinking) criticism is hard on a relationship. Criticism is usually a sign that the criticizing partner has some personal development work to do.

5. SHOW CONTEMPT.

Contempt is criticism escalated to outright mental abuse.

6. REACT DEFENSIVELY.

Fear is natural. Defensiveness naturally accompanies fear. Skillful partnering requires practicing techniques that allow you to drop the defensiveness despite your fear.

7. DENY RESPONSIBILITY.

When you deny responsibility for your part in the issue, you wind up blaming your partner and trying to change him or her.

8. REWRITE HISTORY.

Remembering mainly the negative experiences in a partnership is a predictor for future breakdown. All partnerships have difficult spots.

9. REFUSE TO GET HELP.

Partnership coaching (and willingness) works!

10. BELIEVE THAT CHANGING PARTNERS IS THE SOLUTION.

People may go through several partners while repeatedly avoiding the same basic issues.

MARTY CROUCH
PARTNER COACH

NINE RULES FOR ROMANCE

1.
ONE DATE A WEEK

2.
HOLD HANDS

3.
WALK TOGETHER OUTSIDE

4.
SLOW DANCE TO MUSIC

5.
WATCH ROMANTIC MOVIES

6.
CANDLELIGHT DINNERS AT HOME

7.
WRITE CARDS AND LETTERS

8.
A WEEKEND GETAWAY

9.
TELL YOUR PARTNER WHAT IS ROMANTIC TO YOU

DAVID CLARK, PH.D.
PSYCHOLOGIST AND SEMINAR SPEAKER
FROM "MEN ARE CLAMS AND WOMEN ARE CROWBARS"

10 GREAT ROMANCE MOVIES

1.

AN AFFAIR TO REMEMBER

2.

BEAUTY AND THE BEAST (1940)

3.

CASABLANCA

4.

DOCTOR ZHIVAGO

5.

GONE WITH THE WIND

6.

ROMAN HOLIDAY

7.

SHADOWLANDS

8.

SOMEWHERE IN TIME

9.

THE PHILADELPHIA STORY (1940)

10.

WUTHERING HEIGHTS

COMPILED BY DAN MCAULEY
LONGTIME MOVIE BUFF

SIMPLE WAYS TO BE ROMANTIC

Shower.

Wear perfume/cologne.

Dress nicely.

Floss and brush.

Keep a supply of breath mints, gum, and mouthwash handy.

Hold hands as much as possible.

Whisper "sweet nothings" in each other's ear.

Leave little love notes around the house,
in lunch bags, in cars, in purses.

Call for no reason.

Exercise.

Eat healthy.

Kiss a lot.

Share your deepest desires and dreams.

Be spontaneous.

Put the kids down early, and eat supper late.

Invest in one of those "Romantic Love Songs" CDs.

Buy and burn some scented candles.

Stare into each other's eyes.

Stare into a fire together.

Share a blanket on the couch on a cold night.

Sit side by side on the couch.

Wink at each other.

Hug.

Reminisce about your courtship.

WOODS, HUDSON, DALL, LACKLAND
FROM "MARRIAGE CLUES FOR THE CLUELESS"

TIPS FOR THE ROMANTICALLY CHALLENGED

1.
SHOWER HER WITH PRAISE.
Praise not only affects her,
it changes your perception of her.

2.
TRY NEW THINGS.
Boredom is a mortal enemy to relationships.

3.
ESTABLISH RITUALS.
Romantic rituals ensure that you are
spending quality time together on a regular basis.
If you wait until you are feeling spontaneous
or "in the mood" to be romantic, you
may end up waiting a long time.

4.
GET AWAY!
Don't make the mistake of thinking you can't
afford to take time away—you can't afford not to!

MICHAEL WEBB
CONDENSED FROM "NEW MAN" MAGAZINE

TALK ABOUT THESE THINGS

- What do you think of when you imagine intimacy and closeness?

- What is romance to you? Do you need romance to set the mood for sex?

- What are the positive factors about our love life?

- What brings you the most sexual fulfillment? What do you think brings me the most sexual fulfillment?

- How often would you like to make love?

- How much hugging and cuddling do you need before and after intercourse? (Define this in minutes if necessary.)

- What are the fantasies you have been hoping to fulfill together?

- What changes do we need to make to keep sex fresh and growing?

DAVID AND CLAUDIA ARP
ADAPTED FROM "LOVE LIFE FOR PARENTS" AND "10 GREAT DATES"

13 RULES FOR FIGHTING FAIR

1.
Make an appointment for the discussion.

2.
Face each other.

3.
Keep it limited to one issue.

4.
Keep it respectful.

5.
Keep focused on the present.

6.
Keep focused on understanding first,
being understood second.

7.
Keep focused on the problem, not the person.

8.

Avoid distractions.

9.

Keep it clean.

10.

Keep it tactful.

11.

Take a time-out if needed.

12.

Don't interrupt.

13.

Remember, *your* reality
isn't the only reality.

CAROL CLIFTON, PH.D.
PSYCHOLOGIST

WARNING SIGNS THAT YOUR MARRIAGE NEEDS HELP

Enjoy spending times with others more than partner.

Easily irritated at spouse.

No sexual relations for one month or more.

Easily distracted when mate is talking.

Looking for excuses to stay away from home.

Impatient with partner.

Haven't gone out alone with spouse for a month or more.

Thoughts or threats of divorce.

Believe mate doesn't understand you.

Lack of trust.

Negativity, sarcasm, or criticism toward each other.

Not going to bed at same time (for reasons other than work).

Less communication now than one year ago.

Don't laugh together.

Arguing over the same issue over and over again.

Can't be honest with partner.

Don't enjoy spending time together.

Don't feel respected by spouse.

Bored by relationship.

Haven't given mate a gift in two months or more.

Wondering what it would be like to be married to someone else.

Haven't hugged or cuddled for a month or more (without it leading to sexual relations).

Hard to forgive partner.

Don't know what to talk about when together.

Difficult to think of compliments for mate.

DR. STEVE STEPHENS
PSYCHOLOGIST AND SEMINAR SPEAKER

EIGHT STRATEGIES FOR THE
SECOND HALF OF MARRIAGE

1.
Let go of past marital disappointments, forgive each other,
and commit to making the rest of your marriage the best.

2.
Create a marriage that is partner-focused
rather than child-focused.

3.
Maintain effective communication that allows you
to express your deepest feelings, joys and concerns.

4.
Use anger and conflict creatively to build your relationship.

5.
Build a deeper friendship and enjoy your spouse.

6.
Renew romance and restore a pleasurable sexual relationship.

7.
Adjust to changing roles with aging parents and adult children.

8.
Evaluate where you are on your spiritual pilgrimage.

DAVID AND CLAUDIA ARP
CONDENSED FROM "THE SECOND HALF OF MARRIAGE"

MARRIAGE ADVICE FROM 1886

Let your love be stronger than your
hate or anger.

Learn the wisdom of compromise, for it
is better to bend a little than to break.

Believe the best rather than the worst.

People have a way of living up
or down to your opinion of them.

Remember that true friendship is the
basis for any lasting relationship. The
person you choose to marry is deserving
of the courtesies and kindnesses you
bestow on your friends.

Please hand this down to your children
and your children's children: The more
things change the more they are the same.

JANE WELLS

HOME AND FINANCES

Managing your nest and your nest egg

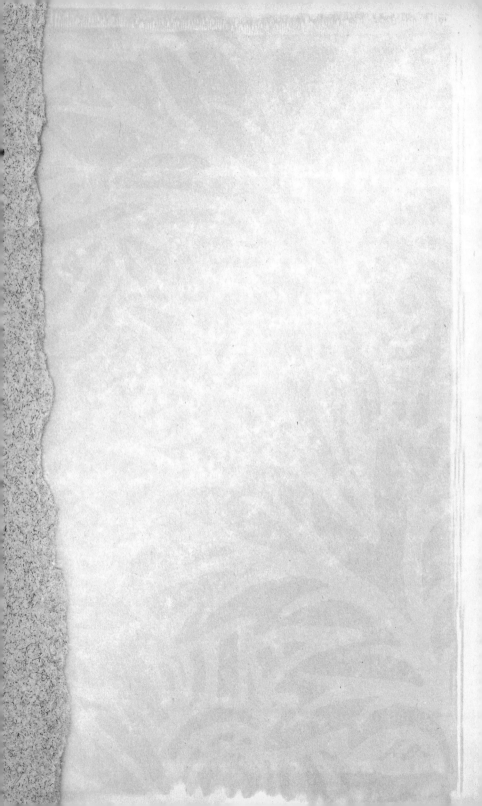

PRINCIPLES FOR DEBT-PROOF LIVING

YOU MUST NEVER KEEP IT ALL
The first thing you must do when money flows
into your life is give some of it away.

YOU MUST NEVER SPEND IT ALL
Always pay yourself before anyone else. Always.

THERE ARE ONLY FIVE THINGS YOU CAN DO WITH MONEY
Give it, save it, invest it, lend it, and spend it.
Notice where spending comes in that lineup: last.
Spending should never be the first thing you do with your money.

PAY CASH
Paying cash requires making some lifestyle changes and
sacrifices, but it will keep you from drowning in a
sea of red ink on your journey to financial freedom.

NO DEBT NO MATTER WHAT
Unsecured debt is like cancer. At first it is not life-threatening
because it involves only a cell or two. But it never stays tiny.

DEVELOP A STRATEGY
Without a plan for getting there, reaching your goal of financial
freedom will remain a dream. A plan turns a dream into a goal.

MARV HUNT
ADAPTED FROM "DEBT-PROOF LIVING"

10 WAYS TO STRETCH
YOUR DOLLARS

1.

Reduce credit-card expense. The goal is really to eliminate credit-card expense. But if you have debts, they may as well cost you as little as possible. Switch to credit cards with the lowest interest rate you can find.

2.

Keep your car after it is paid off. Studies have shown that the cheapest car you can own is the one you already have.

3.

Trim your spending by 2 to 3 percent. It's a small enough amount that you might not even notice the difference.

4.

Save a portion of each increase in income. Try to maintain your existing lifestyle even when your income increases.

5.

Set up your own forced savings plan with money automatically withdrawn at regular intervals from your checking account and deposited in another account.

6.

Use Christmas Clubs or Vacation Clubs to save for large expenses. Money is deducted from your paycheck or bank account each pay period for a year.

7.

Pay cash as often as possible. Studies have shown that people who pay primarily with cash spend less money. It's harder to part with cash than to pull out a credit card.

8.

Give yourself an allowance. Rather than spend everything that's left after giving, saving, and debt paying, limit yourself and your spouse to a weekly allowance that's enough to have fun while still being financially responsible.

9.

Start an empty-wallet policy. If you have allowance money left at the end of the week, save it. I go a step further. Every night I empty my spare change into a big coffee jar.

10.

Don't window-shop. If you do, don't take any money with you, especially a credit card. Even without money, window-shopping is dangerous because it creates desire.

RAY LINDER
ADAPTED FROM "MAKING THE MOST OF YOUR MONEY"

ADVANTAGES TO PAYING CASH

- ❧ Paying cash keeps you focused.

- ❧ Paying cash promotes contentment because it adds meaning and value to the things you do buy.

- ❧ Paying cash lets you own things, not merely acquire them.

- ❧ Paying cash adds meaning and value to the thing purchased.

- ❧ Paying cash makes spending difficult and uncomfortable. And that is exactly the way it should be.

MARY HUNT
FROM "DEBT-PROOF LIVING"

TIPS FOR STAYING WITHIN YOUR BUDGET

DON'T BUY ANYTHING ON IMPULSE.

PAY OFF CREDIT CARDS EACH MONTH.
Charge items only for convenience.

TAKE YOUR LUNCH AND SNACKS TO WORK.
Avoid vending machines.

BUY IN BULK; USE COUPONS.

IF YOU SMOKE, QUIT.
Quitting is good for your health and your budget.

ENTERTAIN AT HOME INSTEAD OF GOING TO A RESTAURANT.

PUT SOME MONEY INTO SAVINGS EVERY PAY PERIOD.
If your company or bank has an automatic savings plan, sign up.

SELECTED FROM "ABOUT...CREATING A BUDGET," A LIFE ADVICE® PAMPHLET
PUBLISHED BY METLIFE'S CONSUMER EDUCATION CENTER

THE SEVEN PILLARS OF
FINANCIAL INDEPENDENCE

THE FIRST PILLAR: AN ATTITUDE OF GRATITUDE

Central to financial freedom is a sincere spirit of thankfulness to God for every big and small blessing in your life. From this heart of gratitude comes the natural, joyful overflow of sharing with your community, church, and worthwhile endeavors around the world.

THE SECOND PILLAR: A COMMITMENT TO HEALTH AND VITALITY

Good health is vital (a) to help avoid big medical expenses down the road and (b) to the fitness, energy, and vitality you will want in order to truly enjoy an active, fulfilling life style.

THE THIRD PILLAR: FREEDOM FROM DEBT

Break and stay free of those *Buy Now, Pay Forever* habits that rob your future as you pay for your past. When you get rid of consumer debt for good, you're liberating thousands of dollars that you can set aside for your future.

THE FOURTH PILLAR: DISCIPLINED SAVINGS

As your consumer-debt load lightens, you'll be able to direct more dollars toward savings for the future. Some of that money should fund a contingency reserve of two to six months' living expenses to help handle life's surprises. Your major savings commitment, however, should be for the long term—so you'll be financially free as you enter your retirement years.

THE FIFTH PILLAR: INVESTING FOR GROWTH

Even the most diligent savers will cheat themselves if they leave all their funds in "safe" places such as bank accounts or certificates of deposit. For long-term retirement savings, put your money to work more aggressively in investments averaging 10 to 12 percent or better annually. You'll be pleasantly surprised at the results over time!

THE SIXTH PILLAR: ASSET PROTECTION

Invest a few dollars now for some "safety nets" to guard against losing what you're working so hard to build. These include important insurance coverages such as adequate life, health, auto, homeowners/renters, and liability coverage. (Warning: Some policies are excellent values while others are wastes of good money. Choose carefully.)

THE SEVENTH PILLAR: MAKING YOUR MONEY LAST

As adults grow older their most prevalent financial fear is: "Will I have enough to 'make it' when I retire? Will I have to move in with my children or depend on the government?" We don't want to merely "survive" financially—we want to thrive! By combining smart planning, savvy investment choices, and systematic withdrawals of funds, we can have all the money we need for as long as we'll need it.

DAN BENSON
FROM "THE NEW RETIREMENT: HOW TO SECURE FINANCIAL
FREEDOM AND LIVE OUT YOUR DREAMS"

DEBT TRAP WARNING SIGNS

1.
You are living on credit.

2.
You pay your bills late.

3.
You are not a giver.

4.
You are not a saver.

5.
You dream of getting rich quickly
and living an extravagant lifestyle.

6.
You worry about money.

7.
You overspend your checking account.

MARY HUNT
CONDENSED FROM "DEBT-PROOF LIVING"

MOST COMMON WAYS TO MISUSE CREDIT CARDS

§ Buying luxuries or nonessentials with credit cards. (Paying for vacations, entertainment, clothes, jewelry, or eating out on credit must be avoided.)

§ Paying the minimum amount due, rather than the entire bill, at the end of the month. (Failing to pay off the credit card bill in full each month is the most common first step toward the debt trap.)

§ Assuming that if we have the credit to buy it, we can afford it. (This is far from the truth.)

§ Accepting a new credit card without paying off the old. (Transferring the credit card balance to a card with a lower interest is wise, but make sure you cancel your old card.)

§ Using a credit card to purchase things that would normally be purchased with cash. (Buying groceries on credit, for instance, is a sign that you are falling into the debt trap.)

BOB RUSSELL
FROM "MONEY: A USER'S MANUAL"

HOW TO BUY A NEW CAR

- Consider the advantages of buying a new car over a used car—warranties, latest engineering features, and a car without an unknown maintenance history.

- Price and financing—Retail price and dealer costs are published in automobile magazines and on the Internet. Determine in advance the maximum you want to spend, and don't budge from that figure.

- Safety and Reliability—Check out safety and crash test results in automobile and consumer magazines.

- Personal Preference—Weigh the advantages and disadvantages of your model choice. Sport Utility Vehicles are durable and offer good visibility but often have less comfort and lower gas mileage. Sports cars have higher insurance costs.

- Extras—There is substantial dealer profit on extras, and they quickly raise the price of your vehicle.

- Decide on at least two makes and models that interest you—Having two choices will help you negotiate more objectively.

READY FOR THE DEALER

- Test drive the two models at the top of your list—Observe handling, visibility, braking, readability of dash instruments, quality of air and radio, comfort of seats, leg room, and storage space.

- Remember the best times to deal—Dealers are usually more willing to deal the last few days of the month. Another good time is just before or after new models come out. Watch for dealer discounts and rebates.

- Show that you are an informed buyer—Let the dealer know you have his invoice cost and that you will buy where you can get the best deal. Negotiate your best price without a trade-in. After you have your price, ask what they will offer you on a trade. Know the approximate value of your car by checking the prices for similar cars in your local newspaper ads.

- Remember—regardless of what the salesman says, a deal is not a sale until it is in writing and signed by both the buyer and the seller.

- It's worth it—Outside of buying a home, a new car is the largest purchase the average family makes. Careful research and intelligent decisions can save thousands of dollars.

HOLT BERTELSON
THE NEW CAR CZAR

HOW TO BUY A USED CAR

1.

Decide how much you can afford to spend before you start shopping. Don't go over that amount.

2.

Determine the value of the car you are considering. Check auto ads or contact lending institutions and ask for the wholesale and retail value. Low mileage, appearance, options, and mechanical conditions are all factors.

3.

Dealer or private party? Your best price is usually through a private party, but a dealer's price may include a warranty or dealer protection. Whenever you buy a newer car, find out if the manufacturer will transfer the unused warranty.

4.

Drive the car in traffic and freeway conditions. Look for problems with steering, vibrations, acceleration, shifting, brakes, engine noise, exhaust, alignment, electrical, ventilation, fluid leaks, and comfort. Look at the car in the daylight.

5.

Demand maintenance records, repair history, and a mechanic's check-up when buying from a private party or "as is" from a dealer. The money you spend on a mechanic can make the difference between buying a gem and a lemon. Ask the seller to put a statement in writing that the odometer has not been changed.

6.

Dicker for your best price. Start with the wholesale value and work up rather than starting from the asking price and working down.

7.

Don't pay cash to a private party unless you get a receipt. Be sure the legal owner signs the release on the car registration form. Don't delay in notifying your car insurance agent.

AL GRAY
CAR COUNSELOR FOR FAMILY AND FRIENDS

CHECKING CURBSIDE APPEAL WHEN SELLING A HOME

- Are the lawn and shrubs well maintained?

- Are there cracks in the foundation or walkways?

- Does the driveway need resurfacing?

- Are the gutters, chimney, and walls in good condition?

- Do the window casings, shutters, siding, or doors need painting?

- Are garbage and debris stored out of sight?

- Are lawn mowers and hoses properly stored?

- Is the garage door closed?

SELECTED FROM "ABOUT...SELLING A HOME," A LIFE ADVICE® PAMPHLET
PUBLISHED BY METLIFE'S CONSUMER EDUCATION CENTER

QUESTIONS TO ASK
BEFORE GETTING A PET

- ♪ What kind of pet do I want?

- ♪ Can I afford the cost of purchasing a pet?

- ♪ Can I afford the cost of caring for a pet (food and grooming, regular health checks, illness)?

- ♪ Do I have time to care for a pet?

- ♪ Do I have the proper environment for the pet?

- ♪ What type of extra housing or equipment will I need for the pet?

- ♪ How will my children handle a new pet?

- ♪ How will other pets in my household react to a new pet?

- ♪ Does anyone in the household have allergies?

SELECTED FROM "ABOUT...CHOOSING AND CARING FOR A PET," A LIFE ADVICE® PAMPHLET
PUBLISHED BY METLIFE'S CONSUMER EDUCATION CENTER

QUALITIES OF A GREAT BABY-SITTER

Shows maturity and common sense

Follows your instructions

Respects your property and rules

Commands your child's obedience

Ensures your child's safety

Responds appropriately to an emergency

Displays love

Plays with your child

Listens to your child

Sets good boundaries

Disciplines in a way you feel comfortable with

Manages their own anger, stress, and frustration

Introduces games and play ideas appropriate to your child

Supports and models your values

Keeps the place picked up

Has good references

TAMI STEPHENS
MOTHER OF THREE

WHAT YOUR BABY-SITTER NEEDS TO KNOW

- Where you will be
- How you might be contacted
- Where a first-aid kit is and how to use it
- Phone numbers to use in an emergency
- Address and cross streets of residence
- Location and use of fire extinguisher
- What and when the children are to eat
- Acceptable television channels and shows that may be watched
- What forms of discipline you wish them to use
- When the children should go to bed
- Bedtime routines and rituals
- Any fears the children have
- Important family rules that must be obeyed
- Expectations as to the children's manners, behaviors, obedience, and tidiness
- Any special allergies or medical problems
- When you will return

TAMI STEPHENS
MOTHER OF THREE

COP'S VACATION CHECKLIST

✓ Discontinue mail and newspaper.

✓ Ask a neighbor or friend to check for packages, flyers, etc.

✓ Ask a neighbor or friend to set out and bring in garbage can.

✓ Have someone check the house each day.

✓ Give key and alarm code to neighbor or family member.

✓ Ask local police or sheriff's department for drive-by checks.

✓ Arrange care for animals.

✓ Leave telephone number where you will be in event of problems.

✓ Set lights on timer.

✓ Arrange to have yard work done.

✓ Turn off water if on extended vacation.

✓ Set heat thermostats.

✓ Close gates, bring toys in, put tools and valuables away.

✓ Put jewelry and money in safe or safety deposit box.

✓ Check refrigerator and freezer doors, making sure they're closed.

✓ Walk through when you leave—check lights and windows, unplug appliances, and turn off computer.

✓ Lock all doors as you walk out.

✓ Take a final look at the house to see if you forgot anything.

KEN MCCLURE
RETIRED POLICE OFFICER

SIX EASY WAYS TO ORGANIZE YOUR KIDS' CLUTTER

A certain degree of clutter is an unavoidable side effect of family life. Here are some tips to help limit the mess in your household.

1. **Create a clutter cache.** If your kids persist in scattering their belongings, collect and place them in a box. Set some ground rules. For example, if your children need an item immediately, they can redeem it by paying a small fine. Otherwise, once each month, let them sort through the box, deciding what to keep and what to discard or give away.

2. **Obtain a large plastic bin for each child.** (Bins that fit under the bed are ideal.) When papers come home from school, allow the student to decide which to keep and which to throw away. A full bin is the limit.

3. **Color-code children's belongings.** Large families especially find this an effective organizational tool. Toothbrush, towel, duffel bag and sheets can be purchased in each child's chosen color. Color-coding makes for easy identification of belongings that need to be put away. It also eliminates some of the bickering over what belongs to whom.

4. ***Cut down on paper clutter*** by recording pertinent information on a calendar as soon as the birthday or invitation or sport information flyer arrives in the mail. Some families use different color markers for each child's events.

5. ***Be selective with purchases.*** For example, bypass school book fairs and visit the public library. If your child finds a book he really likes, then purchase it to place on a shelf with his favorites.

6. ***Install lockers*** (often available secondhand) in the laundry room, garage, or basement. Assign one to each child for the storage of sports equipment, school backpacks, coats, etc.

FAITH TIBBETTS MCDONALD
FROM "VIRTUE" MAGAZINE

22 ITEMS TO ALWAYS CARRY IN YOUR CAR

1.
Jumper cables

2.
First-aid kit

3.
Flashlight

4.
Work gloves

5.
Chains in inclement weather

6.
Fire extinguisher

7.
Flares or reflector triangles

8.
Help sign

9.
Jack (if car is not equipped with one)

10.
Tool kit

11.
Rags

12.
Ice scraper

13.

Tire gauge

14.

Spare tire

15.

Cell phone if driving alone

16.

Container of water

17.

Map

18.

Owner's manual

19.

Car registration

20.

Insurance information

21.

Notepad

22.

Pen or pencil

AL GRAY
A MAN KNOWN FOR BEING PREPARED

CREATE A FAMILY CRAFT BOX

Old shirts for smocks

Old shower curtains for drop cloths

Magazines

Safety scissors

Crayons

Notebooks

Sketchpads

Construction paper

Clothespins

Scrap cloth

Paintbrushes

Glue

Lunch bags

Yarn

Empty food cartons

Colored pencils

Photographs

Popsicle sticks

Tissue paper

Cotton balls

Paint

Newspapers

Twist-ties

Anything else you can find

CONDENSED FROM TRICIA GOYER
FROM "HOMELIFE" MAGAZINE

TEENS

Shaping the future

9

10 GIFTS FOR YOUR TEENS

1.

The gift of time.

2.

The gift of respect.

3.

The gift of hope.

4.

The gift of caring for their friends.

5.

The gift of parameters.

6.

The gift of flexibility.

7.

The gift of understanding.

8.

The gift of other adult friends.

9.

The gift of loving our mates.

10.

The gift of a consistent role model.

SUSAN ALEXANDER YATES
CONDENSED FROM "HOW TO LIKE THE ONES YOU LOVE"

TEENS

HOW WELL DO YOU KNOW
YOUR TEENAGER?

- Who is your teen's best friend?

- What color would he/she like for the walls in his/her bedroom?

- Who is your teen's greatest hero?

- What embarrasses your teen the most?

- What is your teen's biggest fear?

- What is his/her favorite type of music?

- What person outside the immediate family has most influenced your teen?

- What is his/her favorite school subject?

- What is his/her least favorite school subject?

- What has your teen done that he/she feels most proud of?

- What is your teen's biggest complaint about the family?

- What sport does your teen most enjoy?

- What is his/her favorite TV program?

- What really makes your teen angry?

- What would your teen like to be when he/she grows up?

- What chore does your teen like least?

- What three foods does your teen like most?

- What is your teen's most prized possession?

- What is his/her favorite family occasion?

- What activity did your teen enjoy most last weekend?

MIRIAM NEFF
CONDENSED FROM "FAMILYLIFE TODAY"

HOW TO MOTIVATE YOUR TEEN

Teens feel motivated to do right when they have a sense that their parents trust them.

Teens feel motivated to do right when they feel respected by their parents. That is, encouragement works better than put-downs.

Teens feel motivated to do right when their parents live the standard they are being asked to live.

Teens feel motivated to do right when they are given the moral reasons why.

Teens feel motivated to do right when parents are willing to acknowledge their own mistakes instead of make up excuses.

GARY AND ANNE MARIE EZZO
FROM "REACHING THE HEART OF YOUR TEEN"

KIDS WHO RESIST PEER PRESSURE HAVE...

An internal compass of right and wrong.

A fear of God.

General respect for parental and other authority.

A good relationship with their parents.

Self-control, including a willingness to say no to temptations.

Self-esteem.

Self-contentment.

An unwillingness to bend the rules.

A willingness to pay the price when they do make bad choices.

Wisdom to resist tempting environments.

DON S. OTIS
CONDENSED FROM "TEACH YOUR CHILDREN WELL"

FIVE SECRETS OF PARENTING TEENS

1.
CARE ABOUT WHAT MATTERS TO THEM

All teenagers need is the assurance that you have taken notice of their lives, that you have made a special effort to take interest in the things that matter to them. Make their interests your interests.

2.
EMBRACE MOMENTS OF PERSONAL PAIN

Most of the time, heartbreak in a teenager's life seems pretty trite to us. But when painful times hit, it's an open door for you to build trust and respect with your teenager.

3.
PREPARE TO BE TAKEN FOR GRANTED—IT IS WELL WORTH IT

The task of making boys and girls into men and women is not for the feeble at heart. Accept the fact that raising kids means long days and sleepless nights with rare instances of gratitude.

4.
STAY STEADY

More than anything else, teenagers are looking for people who will go the distance with them. They need you to pass the test of time and be there.

5.
PRACTICE MODELING

Whether we realize it or not, our kids are working their lives after ours. Count on it—they take note of everything we do and everything we say.

TED HAGGARD AND JOHN BOLIN
FROM "CONFIDENT PARENTS, EXCEPTIONAL TEENS"

HOW TO RAISE SEXUALLY PURE KIDS

Love them.

Provide them two loving role models.

Teach them who they are.

Teach them moral values.

Keep them active in church.

Help them select their friends.

Warn them about the joys and dangers of sex.

Provide them with clear guidelines for dating.

Teach them moral boundaries.

Help them make a formal commitment to virtue.

Teach them to purify their minds.

Teach them how to say NO!

Watch for signs of sexual involvement.

Provide good reading material that supports your values.

Surround them with prayer.

TIM AND BEVERLY LAHAYE
ADAPTED FROM "RAISING SEXUALLY PURE KIDS"

FOUR WAYS TO STAY SEXUALLY PURE

1.

DON'T PULL DOWN

2.

DON'T PULL UP

3.

DON'T UNZIP

4.

DON'T UNBUTTON

ROBERT JEFFRESS
FROM "SAYING GOODBYE TO REGRET"

TEENS

QUALITIES OF A GOOD TEEN FRIEND

Trustworthiness
Can you trust him when you are not around?

A sense of moral rectitude
Are his actions governed by absolute right or wrong?

The ability to defer gratification
Does your friend regularly resist an impulse?

Respect for authority
Does your friend respect his
parents and other adults?

Honesty
Can you trust him to tell you the truth?

Willingness to forgive
Does he find it easy to let go of the
wrong things others have done to him?

An even temper
When he doesn't get his way,
does he become angry or sullen?

Open-mindedness
Can he handle it when you disagree?

An inquiring mind
Does he strive for personal improvement?

DON S. OTIS
FROM "TEACH YOUR CHILDREN WELL"

TEEN GROUP-DATING IDEAS

- ⚘ Plan a theme party.

- ⚘ Go to a park and participate in outdoor activities.

- ⚘ Make a video.

- ⚘ Have a campfire/bonfire.

- ⚘ Participate in a scavenger hunt (gather items, make a video, or make an audio recording).

- ⚘ Play board/table games.

- ⚘ Attend or participate in athletic contests.

- ⚘ Participate in a trivia challenge.

- ⚘ Play Clue (with real characters)

- ⚘ Work 3-D puzzles.

- ⚘ Cook out.

- ⚘ Coordinate a bike adventure.

- ⚘ Serve others through a ministry project.

JIMMY HESTER
CONDENSED FROM "HOMELIFE" MAGAZINE

HOW TO TEACH RESPECT

SET AN EXAMPLE.

How do you speak about others in your teen's presence? Determine to model respectful attitudes and actions to the youth in your life.

EXPOSE YOUR TEEN TO ETHICAL STANDARDS.

Whether at the dinner table, on the ride home from school, or on a field trip, make your kids aware of their duty to respect all human beings and help them think through why it's important to show an additional measure of respect to parents, elders, teachers and religious and civic authorities.

DEMAND RESPECT FROM YOUR TEENS.

Many parents allow their teens to speak rudely and act indifferently toward one or both parents. While it's certainly wise to pick your battles with a child, you should at the very least expect—and demand—common courtesy and decency.

TREAT KIDS WITH RESPECT.

Don't "talk down" to young people. Don't insult them or call them names. Ask their opinions and listen when they respond. Help them to develop a healthy respect for themselves, and they will be better equipped to respect others.

INSIST THAT SIBLINGS TREAT EACH OTHER WITH RESPECT.

Differences and disagreements may be inevitable among brothers and sisters, but disrespect need not be tolerated. Draw the line at name-calling, insults, and cruel teasing.

CREATE TEACHING OPPORTUNITIES.

Take your teens out on "dates" to teach them how to treat members of the opposite sex with respect and how to accept respectful gestures.

TEACH YOUR TEENS PRACTICAL WAYS TO SHOW RESPECT FOR OTHERS.

Explain manners as ways of communicating respect. Brainstorm practical ways you and your teens can honor the God-given worth of other people.

CONGRATULATE KIDS WHEN YOU SEE OR HEAR THEM ACTING RESPECTFULLY.

Make active attempts to "catch" your teens being respectful (such as offering a chair to Grandma or politely greeting a teacher in the grocery store) and explain why you appreciate and value their behavior.

BOB HOSTETLER
CONDENSED FROM "HOMELIFE" MAGAZINE

WHEN YOUR TEEN FAILS

DON'T BLAME YOURSELF.

Parents cannot be in the physical presence of their teenagers twenty-four hours a day and control their behavior. As frightening as it may seem, your teenager must be given freedom to make decisions.

DON'T PREACH TO THE TEENAGER.

A teenager who has failed needs to wrestle with his own guilt, but he does not need further condemnation.

DON'T TRY TO FIX IT.

If you seek to remove the natural consequences of the teen's failure, you are working against your teen's maturity. Teens learn some of life's deepest lessons through experiencing the consequences of failure.

GIVE YOUR TEENAGER UNCONDITIONAL LOVE.

The wise parent will give love to the teenager no matter what the failure. The teenager needs to know that no matter what he has done, someone is there who still believes in him, who still believes that he is valuable, and who is willing to forgive.

LISTEN TO THE TEENAGER WITH EMPATHY.

Empathy means to enter into the feelings of another. Parents need to put themselves in the shoes of the teenager and try to understand what led to the failure as well as what the teenager is feeling at the moment.

GIVE THE TEENAGER SUPPORT.

Let the teen know that while you do not agree with what he has done and that you cannot remove all the consequences, you will stand by his side as he walks through the process of dealing with the consequences of this failure.

GIVE GUIDANCE TO THE TEENAGER.

The teenager cannot become a responsible adult without having freedom to grapple with his situation and make decisions regarding where he goes from here. Parents who learn how to give this kind of guidance will continue to influence their teenager's decisions in a positive direction.

GARY CHAPMAN
CONDENSED FROM "THE FIVE LOVE LANGUAGES OF TEENAGERS"

MINIMIZE MATERIALISM

- Engage in activities that don't cost much. This reinforces that fun isn't always associated with money.

- Teach your children and show them by your actions that people matter more than things.

- Minimize the exposure to commercial content, including advertisements that appear in your newspaper.

- Keep conversations about major purchases or financial struggles between adults. Children don't need the added stress of knowing about or worrying over financial pressure.

- Beware of "fiction wishing." Don't say, "Wouldn't it be great if we had…?"

- Encourage the deferral of gratification. Encourage your kids to save money in order to purchase something they want instead of just going to the store and buying it for them. Let them know they can't have everything they want and have to make choices.

- Reach out to people in need by volunteering time or services. Visit those in hospitals, nursing homes, or orphanages.

- Encourage your children to save, recycle, reuse, give away, and take care of the material items they have.

- Avoid the temptation of comparing what you or your children have with what others have.

- Explain the difference between functionality and extravagance. For example, designer clothes may not always be better.

- Reject the dress-for-success mentality.

- Talk about the fact that happiness or contentment are rarely the result of what we have. Help your children see that it is what's inside a person that counts, not how many things he or she has.

DON S. OTIS
CONDENSED FROM "TEACH YOUR CHILDREN WELL"

TEENS

WARNING SIGNS THAT MY CHILD IS HEADED FOR TROUBLE

My child may be headed for trouble if he or she...

Becomes lonely, quiet, or moody.

Just seems depressed.

Has very low self-esteem.

Begins having difficulty sleeping.

Seems negative about everything.

Begins to isolate himself or herself.

Is often angry and abusive.

Changes his or her eating habits.

Becomes argumentative and lies to me.

Begins fighting at school and at home.

Begins receiving poor grades.

Begins violating curfew times.

Is arrested for shoplifting.

Drops out of once-loved activities.

Gets caught drinking or taking drugs.

Refuses to go to church anymore.

Becomes lazy and procrastinates regularly.

Dates/befriends kids against my wishes.

Becomes sexually active.

Changes his or her appearance.

Stops making eye contact.

DR. GREG CYNAUMON
ADAPTED FROM "HELPING SINGLE PARENTS WITH TROUBLED KIDS"

WARNING SIGNS OF TEENS HEADED FOR VIOLENT BEHAVIOR

- Grades in school tumble suddenly

- Personality shifts from outgoing to withdrawn

- Fascination with violence, death, blood, and gore, including violent movies, video games, and music laced with violent lyrics

- Intense interest in guns and bombs

- Talking about "getting even" or "settling a score" with some group at school

- Spending time on Web sites that focus on violence or how to build or obtain weapons

- Changes in clothing and hairstyle, including tattoos and paraphernalia associated with gangs or neo-Nazi groups

MARK A. TABB
CONDENSED FROM "HOMELIFE" MAGAZINE

10 COMMANDMENTS FOR TEENAGERS

1.

Live with eternity in mind.

2.

Life is more than friends, money, and material things.

3.

Use your words well.

4.

Use your time well.

5.

Respect your mom and dad.

6.

Value people.

7.

Discipline your sexuality.

8.

Earn your own way.

9.

Tell the truth.

10.

Be grateful for what you have.

TED HAGGARD AND JOHN BOLIN
CONDENSED FROM "CONFIDENT PARENTS, EXCEPTIONAL TEENS"

FAMILY LIFE

Learning and caring together

CHILDREN LEARN WHAT THEY LIVE

If children live with criticism, they learn to condemn.

If children live with hostility, they learn to fight.

If children live with ridicule, they learn to be shy.

If children live with shame, they learn to be guilty.

If children live with encouragement, they learn confidence.

If children live with tolerance, they learn to be patient.

If children live with praise, they learn to appreciate.

If children live with acceptance, they learn to love.

If children live with approval, they learn to like themselves.

If children live with honesty, they learn truthfulness.

*If children live with security, they learn to have
faith in themselves and others.*

*If children live with friendliness, they learn the
world is a nice place in which to live.*

DOROTHY LAW NOLTE
LIBRARIAN

TEACHING THE ABCS
TO YOUR CHILDREN

A lways be on time.

B e a model of honesty.

C are about their hurts.

D o acts of kindness.

E very day give plenty of hugs and kisses.

F orget past offenses.

G ive occasional "token gifts" of love.

H ave a happy disposition—"a merry heart."

I nvest quality time.

J ump for joy when they bring home good grades.

K eep looking for the good and positive.

L isten to their cares and woes and excitement.

M ake adjustments for physical pain.

N ever criticize in front of their peers.

O nly say words that edify.

P ut on the heart of patience.

Q uietly discipline in private.

R ecognize each child is creatively, uniquely different and specially gifted.

S pend time reading to them and listening to them read.

T ake care of yourself.

U nderstand the age-appropriate behavior of each child.

V oicing—teaching them to share facts, thoughts, ideas, dreams, opinions, intuition.

W elcome their friends.

X -ray to the need of the heart.

Y esterday doesn't have to dictate today.

Z oom in on good behavior.

GLENDA HOTTON, M.A.
COUNSELOR

FAMILY LIFE

HELPING YOUR CHILD SUCCEED

§ Help children choose their own goals.

§ Help children imagine the positive results of achieving their own goals and the negative results of not reaching their goals.

§ Remember the power of praise.

§ Expose children to a variety of activities.

§ Expect children to do things right.

§ Believe your children can achieve great things.

§ Help children develop a more positive self-image.

§ Reward your children.

§ Use the ol' "You can do it, can't you?" principle.

§ Be persistent.

§ Be enthusiastic.

§ Develop strong inner convictions.

GARY SMALLEY
FROM "THE KEY TO YOUR CHILD'S HEART"

EVERY PARENT SHOULD ASK...

- What gives my child joy?

- Who is my child's hero?

- What does my child fear most?

- What activities give my child energy?

- Which activities wear my child out?

- If my child got to choose this year's vacation, where would he or she want to go?

- If my child could pick one activity for me to do with him or her, what would it be?

- What music does my child like?

- Other than going to school or sleeping, what does my child spend the most time doing each week?

- What does my child want to be when he or she grows up?

DR. JOHN C. MAXWELL
FROM "BREAKTHROUGH PARENTING"

FAMILY LIFE

25 WAYS TO HELP YOUR CHILD DO BETTER IN SCHOOL

1. Talk positively about school.

2. Develop a relationship with your child's teacher.

3. Attend open house functions.

4. Help out at your child's school.

5. Read with your child.

6. Take your child to the library.

7. Discuss current events.

8. Turn off the TV.

9. Discuss movies, concerts, and books.

10. Discuss your child's homework.

11. Travel with your child.

12. Explore nature with your child.

13. Help your child learn to manage money.

14. Discuss report cards and school reports.

15. Praise your child's progress.

16. Subscribe to periodicals.

17. Use good grammar.

18. Create environments for conversation.

19. Provide good nutrition and sufficient rest.

20. Strengthen your child's memory.

21. Invite interesting adults into your home.

22. Play games and work puzzles.

23. Choose toys that teach well.

24. Provide opportunities for your child to teach.

25. Be your child's biggest school fan.

JAN DARGATZ
CONDENSED FROM "52 WAYS TO HELP YOUR CHILD DO BETTER IN SCHOOL"

13 WAYS TO GET YOUR CHILDREN TO READ

1.
Model reading by having everyone in
the family reading regularly.

2.
Read to your children daily, beginning at birth.

3.
Choose early reading material carefully;
colorful, fun, and age-appropriate.

4.
Show esteem for books by setting aside
shelves or areas just for books.

5.
Purchase some special books such as pop-up books
and books autographed by authors and illustrators.

6.
Buy books on tape; better yet, have a
grandparent read books onto tape.

7.
Subscribe to magazines that keep children's
attention and feed their interest.

8.
Respect children's right to choose what to read,
but also introduce books they may not read on their own.

9.
Regularly visit libraries and bookstores.

10.
Always have good books in the car and take them into
restaurants, offices, etc., for "waiting times."

11.
Set aside part of a child's allowance for a book purchasing fund.

12.
Visit Web sites of children's authors.

13.
Unplug the television.

DORIS HOWARD
LIBRARIAN

FAMILY LIFE

KIDS ONLINE

- $ Never fill out questionnaires or give out personal information.
- $ Never agree to meet in person with anyone without parental presence.
- $ Never enter a chat room without parental supervision.
- $ Never tell anyone where you will be or what you will be doing without parental permission.
- $ Never respond to or send e-mail to new people you meet online.
- $ Never go into a new area online that will cost more money without parental permission.
- $ Never send a photo over the Internet or by mail to anyone you meet online without parental permission.
- $ Never buy or order products online without parental permission.
- $ Never respond to belligerent or suggestive contact that makes you feel uncomfortable.
- $ Always tell your parents when you see something that upsets you, whether you saw it on purpose or by accident.

DONNA RICE HUGHES
FROM "KIDS ONLINE"

SHOWING RESPECT FOR YOUR CHILD

- Accept your child. Respect his developmental ability. Don't compare him to someone else.

- Allow and accept your child's feelings, even anger. Remember, your child has a right to feel his feelings.

- Share your own feelings with your child.

- Don't expect more of your child than you do of yourself.

- Show patience with problems.

- Discipline in private.

- Don't complain about your child or about the burdens of parenting in front of your child.

- Show an interest in his friends. Invite his friends to your house.

- Respect your child's need for privacy.

RON HUTCHCRAFT
FROM "FIVE NEEDS YOUR CHILD MUST HAVE MET AT HOME"

FAMILY LIFE

25 WAYS TO ENJOY YOUR FAMILY

1. Eat dinner together as a family for seven days in a row.
2. Take your wife on a dialogue date.
3. Read your kids a classic book.
4. Memorize the Twenty-third Psalm as a family.
5. Give each family member a hug for twenty-one days in a row (that's how long the experts say it takes to develop a habit).
6. Pick three nights of the week in which the television will remain off.
7. Pray for your spouse and children every day.
8. Plan a vacation together.
9. Take a vacation together.
10. Sit together as a family in church.
11. Take a few hours one afternoon and go to the library as a family.
12. Write each member of your family a letter sharing why you value them.
13. Take each of your children out to breakfast (individually) at least once a month for a year.
14. Help your kids with their homework.
15. Put together a picture puzzle (five hundred pieces or more).

16. Encourage each child to submit to you his most perplexing question, and promise him that you'll either answer it or discuss it with him.

17. Tell your kids how you and your spouse met.

18. Call your wife or husband from work just to see how they're doing.

19. Compile a family tree and teach your children the history of their ancestors.

20. Get involved in a family project that serves or helps someone less fortunate.

21. Spend an evening going through old pictures from family vacations.

22. Praise your spouse and children—in their presence—to someone else.

23. De-clutter your house.

24. Become a monthly supporter of a Third World child.

25. Give each child the freedom to pick his favorite dinner menu at least once a month.

TIM KIMMEL
SELECTED FROM "LITTLE HOUSE ON THE FREEWAY"

THREE WAYS TO KEEP
FAMILY BOUNDARIES

1.
SIMPLIFY THE RULES.

Begin by prioritizing what's essential to you and your family: Everyone is kind to one another, everyone puts dirty clothes in the hamper, everyone takes turns helping in the kitchen. By eliminating the rules that don't matter, you'll have more energy to follow through on those that do.

2.
ENFORCE SAFETY AND HEALTH RULES AND DON'T COMPROMISE.

Everyone washes up before dinner, everyone wears a seat belt in the car, everyone puts his or her toys away when finished playing.

3.
BE CONSISTENT.

If you make a rule, stick with it whether it's the weekend or the busiest day of your week. Your kids will appreciate the boundaries and in the long run, their behavior will reflect it.

DR. MARY MANZ SIMON
CONDENSED FROM "CHRISTIAN PARENTING TODAY" MAGAZINE

TIPS TO CUSTOM-FIT YOUR PARENTING

HANG OUT WITH YOUR KIDS.

You'll learn who shares, who exhibits a big imagination, and who must be active in order to be happy.

OBSERVE YOUR CHILD'S REACTION TO STRESSFUL SITUATIONS.

What frustrates him? What makes him laugh? How does he respond to teasing? Is he tenderhearted or tough?

DISCOVER TALENTS.

Try lessons in piano, art, or karate, and see what develops: an athletic ability or a creative spirit?

OBSERVE YOUR CHILD'S NATURAL SPEED AND CAPACITY FOR LEARNING AND PERFORMING.

Can she handle four things at once, or only one thing at a time? Does she finish projects on time or is she consistently late?

WHAT BRINGS OUT YOUR CHILD'S INQUISITIVE NATURE?

If bugs and spiders mesmerize your daughter, buy her an ant farm. She could be a budding entomologist!

DOTTIE G. BACHTELL
FROM "TODAY'S CHRISTIAN WOMAN" MAGAZINE

THE 10 COMMANDMENTS
OF GRANDPARENTING

1.

Thou shalt not freak out when thy grandchild, to whom
thou has just given a one-half interest in Mt. Rushmore plus two
Oreo cookies, refuses to speak to thee on the telephone.

2.

Thou shalt permit thy grandchildren to have other
grandparents before thee on certain holidays.

3.

Thou shalt honor the father and mother of thy grandchildren,
and thou shalt not substitute thy judgment for theirs.

4.

Thou shalt open the doors of thy home and thy heart to
thy grandchildren without screaming "Don't touch," for thou
knowest that the visit of thy grandchildren shall soon end.

5.

Thou shalt remember thy family history and
teach it diligently unto thy grandchildren.

6.
Thou shalt refrain from exalting the roles of thy grandchildren, remembering always that thy friends also have grandchildren.

7.
Thou shalt not commit effrontery; thou shalt answer the questions of thy grandchildren with dignity and respect.

8.
Thou shalt not steal thy grandchild's witticism and pass it as thine own.

9.
Thou shalt not covet thy neighbor's grandchild for his or her good grades, sweet disposition, or gentle manner.

10.
Thou shalt love thy half-grandchildren, thy step-grandchildren, thy somewhat grandchildren as surely as thou lovest thy natural grandchildren, for it is the heart, not the bloodline, that truly makes thee a grandparent.

DR. LARRY KEEFAUVER
FROM "HUGS FOR GRANDPARENTS"

GOOD TIMES WITH GRANDPARENTS

§ Allow your child to spend time alone with the grandparents. A connection between them is best forged on a one-to-one basis.

§ Don't expect your parents always to agree with the way you are raising your children.

§ When your parents give advice, attempt to listen graciously, even if you decide not to heed it.

§ Keep your children on the sidelines of any conflict. Don't let them feel they are driving a wedge between their parents and grandparents.

§ Let everyone take an occasional break. A trip to the grocery store or a walk with the kids might be the thing everyone needs when tension starts to mount.

§ Keep communication open. Allow room for discussion on parenting styles and the role grandparents play in the lives of their grandchildren.

CYNTHIA SUMNER
FROM "MOMSENSE"

GOLDEN MOMENTS IN A CHILD'S DAY

THE WAKE-UP:

It is important for a child to have some parent-love in the first conscious moment of her day.

THE SENDOFF:

Horses, Olympians, and children run a good race when they get off to a good start. As often as possible, you should be there for breakfast and your child's departure to school.

THE RECEPTION:

If you want to get a real reading on how the "game" went, you have to be there when the "player" comes off the field. Your presence when your child comes in the door says "I love you." Your responsibility at the "reception" is mostly to hug, to listen without judgment, to notice your child is home, and to just be available.

THE DEBRIEFING:

This may come right after The Reception. Kids need to debrief their day—not to be interrogated but to report, celebrate, evaluate, or explode. Again, your role is to listen. Your undivided attention communicates that you care.

THE HAPPY ENDING:

If "all's well that ends well," it's good for a parent to be there at the end of the day. It's a time for an "I love you," an "I'm sorry," or a "thank you." It puts a period on the end of the day.

RON HUTCHCRAFT
FROM "FIVE NEEDS YOUR CHILD MUST HAVE MET AT HOME"

PRINCIPLES OF PARENTING

DEFINE YOUR PRIORITIES.

What's really important to you? Don't spin your wheels on the unimportant things—save your energy for the important issues.

MAKE YOUR LIFE AN EXAMPLE FOR YOUR CHILDREN.

It must be just as much "Be what I am" as it is "Do what I say." Discipline is for parents first. That is why it is so hard.

STUDY YOUR CHILD.

Training your child requires studying him. Know your child. Talk with him. Ask him questions.

BE CAREFUL NOT TO CRUSH YOUR CHILD.

We must never crush his will through verbal or physical intimidation. Our ultimate goal is to train him to choose right for himself, from the heart, even when we aren't around.

TEACH YOUR CHILD TO CONTROL HIMSELF.

Hearing "no" and surviving the frustration that automatically comes with it gives kids strength. It builds endurance and helps them control their frustrations and impulses.

REQUIRE OBEDIENCE.

Say yes whenever you possibly can. But when you say no, mean it. If you must discipline, make the pain of the discipline outweigh the pleasure of disobedience or it will be meaningless to your child.

TEACH RESPECT FOR OTHER PEOPLE AND FOR PROPERTY.

Respect starts in the home. By learning respect at a young age, children see that people and things should not be targets for their wrath.

TEACH HARD WORK.

From a very early age, a child should be a helping member of the family unit. This requires patient, creative, structured teaching. First, you do it for him. Then, you do it together. Finally, he does it himself.

GIVE MANY REWARDS.

Punishment teaches what not to do. You want to teach your child that good and pleasure go together, just as surely as sin and pain. Reward kindness, good deeds, and cheerful obedience.

FORGET GUILT TRIPS.

We all make mistakes, children and parents alike. Children would rather live with a parent who makes an occasional mistake than with one who never cares enough to discipline them at all.

JANI ORTLAND
CONDENSED FROM "FEARLESSLY FEMININE"

STARTING YOUR CHILD ON GOOD HEALTH

Keep safety in mind every minute.

Don't keep handguns at home.

Talk about drugs and sex.

Cut back on television.

Learn CPR.

Stop smoking.

Tell children you love them.

LORAINE STERN, M.D.
CONDENSED FROM "WOMAN'S DAY" MAGAZINE

BUILDING RELATIONSHIPS
WITH YOUR MARRIED KIDS

- Build the relationship with each couple.

- Visit each couple, but not too often.
  And don't stay too long.

- Resist the urge to give advice.

- Tolerate small irritations.

- Be interested in your children's professions,
  hobbies, and activities.

DAVID AND CLAUDIA ARP
FROM "THE SECOND HALF OF MARRIAGE"

10 BEST INDOOR GAMES EVER

1. CHARADES

Each person selects a movie or song title, then has to get others to guess it by acting it out. No words allowed!

2. PING PONG

With two cheap paddles and one ball, you can play on your dining room table. You can even create your own rules, like allowing shots to bounce off the floor or walls.

3. BLOW HOCKEY

Make goals on each end of your kitchen table by placing two pieces of tape a foot apart. Divide into two teams, drop a ping pong ball onto the table, bend over, and start blowing. You score by blowing the ball through your opponent's goal.

4. PILLOW FIGHTS

If you don't occasionally have a gentle pillow fight with your kids, you're missing out on one of the most fun times of all. I suggest one rule: No hitting on the head. Anyone who violates that rule must sit out the rest of the fight.

5. PAPER PLANES

Help your kids fold paper airplanes and see whose goes the farthest. Then place a target on the rug and see how close everyone can come to landing on it.

6. FICKLE FEATHER

Have everyone kneel in a circle and pull a bedsheet taut, holding it in place with your chins. Place a feather on the sheet and try to blow it away from your side. Score a point for each time it drops on your side—fewest points wins.

7. TABLE HOCKEY

Position one person on each side of your dining room table, then drop a tennis ball in the middle. Players bat the ball to try to send it past an opponent. If it goes off your side, you're assessed a point. The ball must *roll* off the edge—no throwing. Low score wins.

8. BALLOON BLAST

Divide a room into halves with string, make two teams, and bat a balloon around. The purpose is to keep the balloon from falling on your side.

9. BALLOON SOCCER

Take off your shoes and use a balloon as a soccer ball, marking out two "goals" in your living room. No hands allowed—but have plenty of extra balloons ready!

10. FOLLOW THE LEADER

One person leads the family in funny actions (hop on one foot, rub your belly, etc.). Everyone else must follow him exactly.

JERRY AND PATTI MACGREGOR
CONDENSED FROM "FAMILY TIMES"

FAMILY LOVE

Bonding together

A PARENT'S COMMITMENT

§ We are committed to help them be successful
in whatever they want to do.

§ We will be committed to them after they
are married.

§ We will be committed to them no matter whom
they marry.

§ We will be committed to them no matter what
happens during their marriage.

§ We will be committed to their mates and to
their children.

§ We will always be available to listen.

§ Should they get into trouble, we will be there
to help.

GARY SMALLEY AND JOHN TRENT
FROM "LEAVING THE LIGHT ON"

25 SIMPLE WAYS TO TELL YOUR CHILD "I LOVE YOU"

1.
Make a pledge to love your child.

2.
Meet your child's basic needs.

3.
Use loving nicknames.

4.
Read with your child.

5.
Make something together.

6.
Keep your child's secrets.

7.
Keep a special place for memories of your child.

8.
Get down on your child's level.

9.
Find something to do for mutual fun.

10.
Just tell them "I love you."

11.
Give hugs and kisses.

12.
Be willing to let go.

13.
Leave surprise notes and messages.

14.

Give your child heirloom items.

15.

Have a listening ear.

16.

Send a card.

17.

Apologize when you need to.

18.

Take time to play with your child.

19.

Take your child with you.

20.

Have a "date" with your child.

21.

Display your child's photograph.

22.

Help your child build a collection.

23.

Set rules.

24.

Pray for your child.

25.

Protect your child.

JAN DARGATZ
CONDENSED FROM "52 SIMPLE WAYS TO TELL YOUR CHILD 'I LOVE YOU'"

HOME RULES

Always be honest.

Count your blessings.

Bear each other's burdens.

Forgive and forget.

Be kind and tenderhearted.

Comfort one another.

Keep your promises.

Be supportive of one another.

Be true to each other.

Look after each other.

Treat each other as you treat your friends.

But most important
Love one another deeply from the heart.

SELECTED FROM THE HOLY BIBLE

A PARENT'S DAILY PRAYER GUIDE

MONDAY:

Ask God to place a protective, solid hedge around your children.

TUESDAY:

Pray that your children would use godly wisdom in selecting
friends and peers who will make a positive difference in their lives.

WEDNESDAY:

Pray that your children would stay pure in their thoughts and deeds.

THURSDAY:

Pray that they will be caught if they
wander into cheating, lies, or mischief.

FRIDAY:

Pray that they will be alert and thinking clearly as they attend school
and extracurricular activities, and as they take exams.

SATURDAY:

Pray for the spouse each child will marry someday.

SUNDAY:

Ask God to help them live their lives for Him.

DON AND SUE MYERS
CONDENSED FROM "REAL FAMILYLIFE" MAGAZINE

WAYS TO MAKE YOUR MOM FEEL SPECIAL

1. Create a song to honor your mom.

2. Leave little thank-you notes in unusual places.

3. Ask your mom to tell you about experiences she had when she was a little girl.

4. Hug your mom and tell her, "I love you."

5. Offer to help Mom around the house in addition to your "job list."

6. Pray for your mom often.

7. Make a bookmark and put it in a book she is reading.

8. Say "I love you" each day to your mother.

9. Cut out magazine pictures of activities your mom likes to do and make a poster collage.

10. Make a banner with a slogan telling her about a special talent you appreciate, such as "My Mom's a Champion Pie Baker!"

11. When you pray as a family, thank God for your mother and ask Him to bless her in special ways.

12. Make a greeting card with a personal message. Write three things you love about your mom.

13. Talk with Mom about happy experiences you've shared.

CHARLOTTE ADELSPERGER
CONDENSED FROM "FOCUS ON THE FAMILY 'CLUBHOUSE'"

WAYS TO HONOR YOUR DAD

- Seek his wisdom.

- Honor his legacy.

- Explore his family history.

- Show him respect.

- Express love.

- Celebrate Father's Day.

- Remember his birthday.

- Honor his wife.

- Pray for him daily.

- Build a memory book.

- Respect his preferences.

- Surprise him with a special gift.

- Take him fishing.

JOHN VAN DIEST
FATHER OF THREE, GRANDFATHER OF NINE

AFFIRMING YOUR CHILDREN

PRAISE SELECTIVELY.

Indiscriminate praise doesn't motivate; it only confuses. When your child is disruptive or disrespectful, resist the myth that says children learn obedience by flattery. Praise only when behavior or character reflects your desires.

PRAISE IMMEDIATELY.

Delayed praise has less meaning than immediate praise. When you praise a child hours after a good choice was made, he may not remember the action. Catch your little ones "in the act" of doing something praiseworthy, and then respond immediately.

PRAISE SPECIFICALLY.

When you praise your child, assign your praise to noticeable acts or attitudes. "I like the way you shared your toy!" "What a good job you did making your bed today!" "Look at you. You remembered to brush your teeth all by yourself!"

PRAISE INTENTIONALLY.

Look for ways to praise your child. When your daughter brings you a finger painting, look carefully for something you like in it (maybe the colors are mostly mud-like, but notice the smudge of bright yellow). Single out what you like and then display the piece on the refrigerator or a bulletin board. When you're going about your daily chores and you notice your toddler occupying himself with a puzzle, tell him how proud you are of his choice to play alone sometimes.

ELISA MORGAN AND CAROL KUYKENDALL
FROM "WHAT EVERY CHILD NEEDS"

MESSAGES THAT LAST A LIFETIME

"I belong."
Those hours in your arms give your baby the
message, "I am loved. Somebody's there for me."

"I'm special."
It is never too early to begin affirming
your baby and letting her know how
valuable she is in God's eyes and in your heart.

"I trust."
Because in his distress you comfort him,
your baby learns…that you will
respond and are worthy of his trust.

"I can."
Applaud your baby's milestones. Show
your joy as he stretches his little body and his mind.

WILLIAM SEARS, MARTHA SEARS, JOYCE WARMAN, ET AL.
FROM "PARENT PROJECT: TOOLS FOR GODLY PARENTING"

10 GIFTS TO GIVE YOUR CHILDREN

1. LOVE

Every child wants love, and it's so easy to love a child.

2. DISCIPLINE

No parent likes to come home to the role of disciplinarian, yet that's exactly what your child needs from you—the strong, sure limits you provide.

3. A GOOD EXAMPLE

The most important messages you convey to your children are the unspoken ones.

4. RESPECT

A child needs your respect in order to develop self-respect.

5. A GOOD SELF-IMAGE

Love and respect enhance a child's self image, but try not to over-praise or hover. Compliments for a job well done are great, but when praise is undeserved, a child knows it, and that can undermine her self-image.

6. GOOD HEALTH HABITS

Start early to guard his health with preventive healthcare visits. Take care of yourself too: always brushing your teeth, exercising, and eating healthful snacks are the surest ways to install in your child the value of taking good care of his own body.

7. TIME TOGETHER

Even though life is busy and complicated, make sure your child knows that she comes first. You need to be available to her at mealtimes, on weekends, and for school functions. Bathtime and bedtime rituals are also important, as is sharing sports, music, and fun.

8. MOTIVATION FOR LEARNING

All parents who are concerned about learning naturally model that drive for their children, but the danger is in pushing them beyond their limits.

9. SENSE OF HUMOR

Laugh with your children so they can see the light and joyful side of things. Humor may not come easily when you're feeling stressed, but try not to be too serious. Laughter gives us balance.

10. PEER RELATIONSHIPS

From the second year on, a child needs playmates. Through play with children his own age or slightly older, he learns about compromise and empathy; he develops new skills, interests and responsibility to others.

T. BERRY BRAZELTON, M.D.
CONDENSED FROM "FAMILY CIRCLE" MAGAZINE

MAXIMIZE YOUR GRANDPARENTING SKILLS

Love each child equally.

Give gentle hugs and hold hands.

Be good listeners.

Read and tell good stories.

Know basic first aid.

Be supportive of the child's parents.

Look for teachable moments.

Have a cheerful attitude.

Tell children positive traits you see in them.

Remember birthdays and special occasions.

Initiate fun ideas and activities.

Play table games.

Keep regular contact by visits, phone calls, and letters.

Pray regularly.

Spoil a little but not too much.

JOHN VAN DIEST
GRANDFATHER OF NINE

I REMEMBER GRANDMA AND GRANDPA BECAUSE...

They read to me and let me read to them.

They liked my turtle and tree house.

They told interesting stories from their childhood.

They helped me with hard jobs.

They liked spinach!

They saw things I didn't (like good things about my brother).

They taught me how to save, give, and spend money.

They had special names for me.

They gave me their full attention.

*They had rules to live by, and I knew
what they were just by being with them.*

They sent "snail mail" cards.

They thought I was special.

PAT VAN DIEST
GRANDMOTHER OF NINE

FAMILY LOVE

TRAITS OF A LOVING FAMILY

A LOVING FAMILY...

- 𝕾 Communicates and listens.
- 𝕾 Affirms and supports each other.
- 𝕾 Teaches respect for each other.
- 𝕾 Develops a sense of trust.
- 𝕾 Has a sense of play and humor.
- 𝕾 Exhibits a sense of shared responsibility.
- 𝕾 Teaches a sense of right and wrong.
- 𝕾 Has a strong sense of family in which rituals and traditions abound.
- 𝕾 Has a balance of interaction among members.
- 𝕾 Has a shared religious core.
- 𝕾 Respects the privacy of one another.
- 𝕾 Values service to others.
- 𝕾 Fosters table time and conversation.
- 𝕾 Shares leisure time.
- 𝕾 Admits to and seeks help with problems.

DOLORES CURRAN
FROM "TRAITS OF A HEALTHY FAMILY"

FOUR FOUNDATION STONES
OF PARENTAL LOVE

1.

Meeting the emotional and
nurturance needs of your child

2.

Giving loving training and
discipline to your child

3.

Providing physical and emotional
protection for your child

4.

Teaching and modeling anger
management for your child

DR. ROSS CAMPBELL
FROM "RELATIONAL PARENTING"

FAMILY LOVE

KEEP COMMUNICATION
OPEN WITH YOUR CHILD

- Ask your child what his or her favorite song is, listen to it, go over the words, discuss what they mean, and ask what makes the song a favorite.

- Break through superficial conversation by asking some probing questions: "What's going well in your life? What's not going well? What changes would you like to make? What is the biggest challenge you're currently facing?"

- Ask your child to pick a new sport, hobby, art project, or interest for the two of you to develop together.

- Keep a journal of family highlights and special accomplishments throughout the year. Review it together on December 31.

- Help your child develop a set of lifetime goals.

- Share some of the struggles you had when you were your child's age (this may require some digging in your memory!). Then ask your child what his or her struggles are.

- Ask your child to pick three places within driving distance that he or she wants to visit, and make a plan to see them during the next year.

- Take your child to work or the place you volunteer for a day.

- Adopt a grandparent in a nursing home.

- Ask your child about his or her heroes. Write a letter to the person and see if you get a response.

- Tell your child your family history while he or she records it on cassette tape or videotape.

- Research the meaning of your child's name and point out the character traits that parallel the name.

- Write your child a letter saying what in your life you enjoy, what you don't, how you have succeeded, where you made mistakes, and what you hope he or she can learn from your life.

- Serve at a soup kitchen together.

- Play board games or cards with your child. Use this time to find out what's going on in his or her life.

STEPHEN ARTERBURN AND JIM BURNS
CONDENSED FROM "PARENTS GUIDE TO TOP 10 DANGERS TEENS FACE"

FAMILY LOVE

SIX QUESTIONS TO GET
YOUR KIDS TALKING

1.

What's one thing I could pray
for you about this week?

2.

If you could be anything when
you grow up, what would you be?

3.

What's one thing you really appreciate
about your best friend?

4.

If we could go anywhere on vacation,
where would we go and what would we do?

5.

What's your favorite thing for us to do as a
family that doesn't involve spending money?

6.

What's one thing I could work on that
would make you feel even more loved?

JOHN TRENT, PH.D.
FROM "CHRISTIAN PARENTING TODAY"

GIVING LOVE TO CHILDREN

GIVE THE CHOICE OF LOVE.

Commit to love because it is right, not because it feels good.

GIVE THE WORDS OF LOVE.

We all need regular verbal assurance, but children need it the most.

GIVE THE TOUCH OF LOVE.

Research has confirmed the human need for physical touch.
The need to be held and cuddled is especially critical for babies.

GIVE THE ENCOURAGEMENT OF LOVE.

"Put courage into" those little people by letting them
know that you are their best fan and cheerleader.

GIVE THE COMFORT OF LOVE.

In times of pain or sadness, love offers healing comfort.

GIVE THE LAUGHTER OF LOVE.

Laughter sets a pleasant mood, a bright tone.
Make merriment a daily dose of love in your home.

GIVE THE DISCIPLINE OF LOVE.

Discipline establishes boundaries for children,
making them feel safe and secure.

DONNA OTTO
FROM "THE GENTLE ART OF MENTORING"

BOLSTERING YOUR CHILD'S CONFIDENCE

NOTICE AND AFFIRM WHEN THEY DO WELL:

"Your words showed understanding. I'm proud of the way you cared for your friend."

FIND STRENGTHS RELATED TO EVERY WEAKNESS:

"You ran hard after that soccer ball!" rather than "Why can't you learn how to kick the ball properly!"

DOWNPLAY CRITICISM. WHEN YOU HAVE TO CRITICIZE, FOCUS ON THE ACTION RATHER THAN THE CHILD:

"Being late makes it hard to trust you," rather than "You're always late! I'll never be able to trust you again!"

POINT OUT SOMETHING POSITIVE ABOUT FRUSTRATIONS:

"Even though you were late, you did call. That shows consideration and a sense of responsibility."

HELP CHILDREN SOLVE THEIR OWN PROBLEMS:

"How might we master this lateness problem? I know it's as frustrating for you as it is for me." Together with your child, list several possibilities and implement one.

GUIDE YOUR CHILDREN IN EVALUATING THEIR ACTIONS. ASK:

"What went well in your plan?" "What might we have done even better?" "What action would you change if you could do it again?"

KAREN DOCKREY
FROM "PARENTING: QUESTIONS WOMEN ASK"

WISDOM

Learning from the experience of others

12

SEVEN LESSONS FOR LIVING

1.
Don't waste.

2.
Work hard.

3.
Don't cut corners.

4.
Have fun doing things.

5.
Be strict but caring.

6.
Tackle problems head-on.

7.
Pray.

GRANDMA SINCLAIR, GRANDMOTHER OF DAVE THOMAS (WENDY'S)
FROM "WELL DONE!"

LESSONS FROM AESOP'S FABLES

Avoid solutions that are worse than the problem.

It is great art to do the right thing at the right time.

Example is more powerful than reproach.

Honesty is the best policy.

He who is discontented in one place will seldom be happy in another.

Do boldly what you do at all.

The worth of money is not in its possession, but in its use.

Those who seek to please everybody, please no one.

The memory of a good deed lives on.

Happy is the man who learns from the misfortunes of others.

He who wishes evil for his neighbor brings a curse upon himself.

Do not attempt too much at once.

AESOP
ANCIENT STORYTELLER

WISE SAYINGS MY MOTHER TAUGHT ME

A thing of beauty is a joy forever.

It's always darkest just before the dawn.

Big oaks from little acorns grow.

God never gives more than you can bear.

This, too, shall pass.

Can't never did anything.

Nothing ventured, nothing gained.

A man is known by the friends he keeps.

Still waters run deep.

All the flowers of tomorrow are in the seeds of today.

NOLA BERTELSON
MOTHER AND GRANDMOTHER

A FATHER'S ADVICE

- Make God and people your top priority.

- Stop and smell the roses.

- Keep your promises.

- Persevere. Life is tough. Period.

- Express yourself.

- Remember that God molds our character through discomfort, through challenge.

- Choose your friends wisely.

- Let your actions speak louder than your words.

§ Remember your roots.

§ Laugh, often and loud.

§ Learn to discern right from wrong.

§ Don't be afraid to say you're sorry.

§ Pray.

§ Read. Read. Read.

§ Humility is a greater virtue than pride.

BOB WELCH
ADAPTED FROM "A FATHER FOR ALL SEASONS"

WISDOM

DO GOOD

Hate evil.

Cling to what is good.

Devote yourself to brotherly love.

Honor one another.

Be joyful.

Share with those in need.

Practice hospitality.

Rejoice with those who rejoice.

Mourn with those who mourn.

Avoid pride.

Do what is right.

Live at peace with one another.

Seek not revenge.

Do not be overcome by evil.

Overcome evil with good.

ST. PAUL
ADAPTED FROM ROMANS 12:9–21

Life may change,
but it may fly not;

Hope may vanish,
but can die not!

Truth be veiled,
but still it burneth;

Love repulsed,
but it returneth!

PERCY BYSSHE SHELLEY
POET

10 RULES TO LIVE BY

1.
Count your blessings.

2.
Today, and every day, deliver more
than you are getting paid to do.

3.
Whenever you make a mistake or
get knocked down by life,
don't look back at it too long.

4.
Always reward your long hours of
labor and toil in the very best
way, surrounded by your family.

5.
Build this day on a foundation
of pleasant thoughts.

6.

Live this day as if it will be your last.

7.

Laugh at yourself and at life.

8.

Never neglect the little things.

9.

Welcome every morning with a smile.

10.

Search for the seed of good in every adversity.

OG MANDINO
FROM "A BETTER WAY TO LIVE"

WISDOM

KIDS SAY THE WISEST THINGS

- If you want someone to listen to you, whisper it.

- You can't be everyone's best friend.

- All libraries smell the same.

- Sometimes you have to take the test before you've finished studying.

- Silence can be an answer.

- Ask where things come from.

- If you throw a ball at someone, they'll probably throw it back.

- Don't nod on the phone.

- Say grace.

- The best place to be when you are sad is in Grandma's lap.

PHIL CALLAWAY
FROM "WHO PUT THE SKUNK IN THE TRUNK?"

THE WISDOM OF ABRAHAM LINCOLN

- You are only what you are when no one is looking.

- Character is like a tree, and reputation is like a shadow.
  The shadow is what we think of it; the tree is the real thing.

- I have simply tried to do what seemed
  best each day, as each day came.

- To sit by in silence, when they should protest,
  makes cowards of men.

- It often requires more courage to dare to do right,
  than to fear to do wrong.

- Those who deny freedom to others deserve it not for
  themselves. And, under a just God, cannot long retain it.

- The better part of one's life consists of his friendships.

- It is more important to know that we are on God's side.

- A good laugh is good for both the mental and physical digestion.

- You cannot help men permanently by doing for
  them what they could and should do for themselves.

- Nearly all men can stand adversity, but if you
  want to test a man's character, give him power.

- Let minor differences and personal preferences,
  if there be such, go to the winds.

ABRAHAM LINCOLN
16TH PRESIDENT OF THE UNITED STATES

10 SECRETS TO AGELESS LIVING

1.

Never let age get in the way of life.

2.

Stay curious, explore, discover,
and continue to learn new things.

3.

Play, have fun, be happy, and maintain
a zest for life by being vital.

4.

Keep the brain and the body busy;
stimulate the mind, eat healthy, exercise.

5.

Smile, laugh, maintain a sense of humor,
and always stay young at heart.

6.

Have a positive attitude, outlook,
and be optimistic to overcome challenges.

7.

Believe in yourself by having faith,
hope, spirit, value, meaning, and purpose.

8.

Stay connected, engaged, creative,
and useful by continuing to contribute.

9.

Find fulfillment, peace, serenity, and self-esteem
by giving back—volunteer.

10.

Enjoy and cherish healthy relationships
with loved ones, friends, and family.

KELLY FERRIN
FROM "WHAT'S AGE GOT TO DO WITH IT?"

PRACTICAL WORDS
OF A PHILOSOPHER

Be gracious.

Know your chief asset and cultivate it.

Never exaggerate.

Do nothing to make you lose respect for yourself.

Have strength of spirit.

Work with good tools.

Keep in mind the happy ending.

To jog the understanding is a greater feat than to jog the memory.

Know how to refuse.

Be alert when seeking information.

Forestall evil gossip.

Be generous in action.

Have a just estimate of yourself.

Attain and maintain a good reputation.

Do not make a show of what you have.

The shortest road to being somebody is to know whom to follow.

Prepare yourself in good fortune, for the bad.

Do not a business of the trivial.

Never cry about your woes.

Know the value of reconsideration.

BALTASAR GRACIAN
PHILOSOPHER

WISDOM

VANITY

It is vanity to seek material wealth that cannot last and to place your trust in it.

It is also vanity to seek recognition and status.

It is vanity to chase after what the world says you should want and to long for things you should not have, things that you will pay a high price for later on if you get them.

It is vanity to wish for a long life and to care little about a good life.

It is vanity to focus only on your present life and not to look ahead to your future life.

It is vanity to live for the joys of the moment and not to seek eagerly the lasting joys that await you.

THOMAS Á KEMPIS
FROM "THE IMITATION OF CHRIST"

SEIZE THE DAY...

- When you have the choice between taking an escalator or the stairs, take the stairs.

- Place fresh flowers in the places where you live and work.

- Visit the Holy Land once in your life.

- Smile at babies.

- When you develop your film, get double prints. Give the duplicates away.

- Remember, there is time for love and a place for love. Any time, any place.

- Always go the extra mile...whether for a friend or mint chocolate ice cream.

- Whenever you look back on your life, be positive.

- If you seek wisdom over opportunity, opportunity will usually follow.

- Change is a process, not an event.

- Plan to be spontaneous.

- Whenever you look ahead, be optimistic.

- Enjoy each day as if it were your last.

BRUCE BICKEL AND STAN JANTZ
FROM "GOD IS IN THE SMALL STUFF: AND IT ALL MATTERS"

WISDOM

12 LESSONS WORTH REPEATING

1.

Be honest.

2.

Set goals and work quietly
and systematically toward them.

3.

Assign a task to yourself.

4.

Never give up.

5.

Be confident that you can make a difference.

6.

Don't ever stop learning and improving.

7.

Slow down and live.

8.

Choose your friends carefully.

9.

Be a can-do and will-try person.

10.

Try to live in the present.

11.

You are in charge of your own attitude.

12.

Always remember that you are never alone.

MARIAN WRIGHT EDELMAN
CONDENSED FROM "THE MEASURE OF OUR SUCCESS"

BE

Be understanding to your enemies,

Be loyal to your friends.

Be strong enough to face the world each day.

Be weak enough to know you cannot do everything alone.

Be generous to those who need your help.

Be frugal with what you need yourself.

Be wise enough to know that you do not know everything.

Be foolish enough to believe in miracles.

Be willing to share your joys.

Be willing to share the sorrows of others.

Be a leader when you see a path others have missed.

Be a follower when you are shrouded by the mists of uncertainty.

Be the first to congratulate an opponent who succeeds.

Be the last to criticize a colleague who fails.

Be sure where your next step will fall, so that you will not tumble.

Be sure of your final destination, in case you are going the wrong way.

Be loving to those who do not love you, and they may change.

Above all, be yourself.

AUTHOR UNKNOWN

FEAR AND FAITH

Fear imprisons. *Faith frees.*

Fear troubles. *Faith triumphs.*

Fear cowers. *Faith empowers.*

Fear disheartens. *Faith encourages.*

Fear darkens. *Faith brightens.*

Fear cripples. *Faith heals.*

Fear puts hopelessness *Faith puts fear at*
at the center of life. *the feet of God.*

PHIL CALLAWAY
FROM "WHO PUT THE SKUNK IN THE TRUNK?"

If you don't have a Bible, GET ONE.

If you've got a Bible, READ IT.

If you read the Bible, BELIEVE IT.

If you believe the Bible, LIVE IT.

BRUCE AND CHERYL BICKEL AND STAN AND KARIN JANTZ
FROM "LIFE'S LITTLE HANDBOOK OF WISDOM"

Beyond Information...
Inspiration!

SUCCESS · FRIENDSHIP · VIRTUE · MARRIAGE · HOME
HEALTH · CONTENTMENT · LOVE · FAMILY · WISDOM

LISTS
to live by

For everything that really matters.

COMPILED BY
ALICE GRAY STEVE STEPHENS JOHN VAN DIEST

This treasury of to-the-point inspiration—two hundred lists—is loaded with invaluable insights for wives, husbands, kids, teens, friends, and more. These wide-ranging ideas can change your life, and the lives of those you share them with!

ISBN 1-57673-478-1

Books compiled by
Alice Gray

Stories for the Extreme Teen's Heart ISBN 1-57673-703-9

Stories for a Teen's Heart ISBN 1-57673-646-6

Stories for a Kindred Heart ISBN 1-57673-704-7

Stories for a Faithful Heart ISBN 1-57673-491-9

Stories for a Woman's Heart ISBN 1-57673-474-9

Stories for the Family's Heart ISBN 1-57673-356-4

Stories for a Man's Heart ISBN 1-57673-479-X

Stories for the Heart, **The Original Collection**
ISBN 1-57673-127-8

Stories for the Heart, **The Second Collection**
ISBN 1-57673-823-X

More than 4
million sold
in series!

Books compiled by
John Van Diest

Unsolved Miracles

Nothing shows God's awesome love and power like a miracle. *Unsolved Miracles* is an extraordinary collection of uplifting stories that reveal God's wondrous and enduring love.

ISBN 1-57673-226-6

Ten Answers to Life's Most Perplexing Problems

Money. Self-worth. Decision-making. Marriage. Today's top Christian leaders offer solutions to the biggest concerns of our times.

ISBN 1-57673-302-5

ACKNOWLEDGMENTS

More than a thousand books and magazines were researched and dozens of professionals interviewed for this collection. A diligent effort has been made to attribute original ownership of each list, and when necessary, obtain permission to reprint. If we have overlooked giving proper credit to anyone, please accept our apologies. If you will contact Multnomah Publishers, Inc., Post Office Box 1720, Sisters, Oregon 97759, with written documentation, corrections will be made prior to additional printings.

Notes and acknowledgments are shown in the order the lists appear in each section of the book. For permission to reprint a list, please request permission from the original source shown in the following bibliography. The editors gratefully acknowledge authors, publishers, and agents who granted permission for reprinting these lists.

SUCCESS

"Seven Favorite Quotations of Zig Ziglar" by Zig Ziglar, author and motivational teacher, condensed from *Christian Reader* magazine, May/June 2000. Used by permission of the author.

"Persistence" by Charles Stanley from *In Touch* magazine, January 2000, In Touch Ministries, Atlanta, GA. Used by permission of the author.

"Three Great Essentials" by Thomas Edison.

"20 Power Thoughts" from *Power Thoughts* by Robert H. Schuller. Copyright © 1993 by Robert Schuller. Reprinted by permission of HarperCollins Publishers, Inc.

"People Who Make a Difference Have..." by Charles R. Swindoll from *The Tale of the Tardy Oxcart*, Charles R. Swindoll, © 1998, Word Publishing, Nashville, Tennessee. All rights reserved.

"Thoughts That Hold Us Back" by John Van Diest, associate publisher. Used by permission.

"Effective Leaders" taken from *Things Only Men Know*. Copyright © 1999 by Preston Gillham. Published by Harvest House Publishers, Eugene, Oregon 97402. Used by permission.

"Don'ts for Decision Making" from *Healing the Hurting Heart* by June Hunt. Used by permission of the author. June Hunt is host of two international radio ministries, Hope for the Heart and Hope in the Night, located in Dallas, Texas. Author and speaker on biblical counseling, June communicates God's Truth for Today's Problems.

"Are You a Good Time Manager?" condensed from *Tyme Management*™ by Rutherford Publishing, Inc. The *Tyme Management*™ newsletter provides time management tips and suggestions to those in the workforce. For more information, visit www.rpublish.com. Copyright 2000 Rutherford Publishing, Inc. All rights reserved.

"Smart Goals Are..." by Alice Gray, Dr. Steve Stephens, and John Van Diest. Used by permission of the authors.

"Criticism Kills..." by Dr. Steve Stephens, Clackamas, Oregon. Used by permission of the author.

"Six-Step Recipe for Success" by Jeffrey Gitomer from *Women as Managers*, Vol. 98/No. 1, copyright © 1998, The Economics Press, Inc. Reprinted by permission. Copyright © 1998, *Women as Managers*,

The Economics Press, Inc., 12 Daniel Rd., Fairfield, NJ 07004-2565; Phone: 800-526-2554. FAX: 973-227-9742. E-mail: info@epinc.com Web site: www.epinc.com.

"Five Keys to Conversation" taken from *Confident Parents, Exceptional Teens* by Ted Haggard and John Bolin. Copyright © 1999 by Ted Haggard and John Bolin. Used by permission of Zondervan Publishing House.

"The Ten Commandments of Giving a Speech" by Steve Brown condensed from *How to Talk So People Will Listen*. Used by permission of Baker Book House, Grand Rapids, Michigan, © 1999.

STEPPING FORWARD

"Three Pillars of Learning" by Benjamin Disraeli.

"Seven Lessons to Learn" by John Van Diest, associate publisher. Used by permission of the author.

"Seven Important Choices" by Sheri Rose Shepherd from *7 Ways to a Better You*. Published by Multnomah Publishers, Inc., Sisters, OR, © 1999. Used by permission.

"Living Like There's No Tomorrow" by Jeff Herring from the *Oregonian* newspaper, Saturday, April 3, 1999. Reprinted with permission of Knight Ridder/Tribune Information Services.

"Seven Ways to Make Yourself Miserable" by Elisabeth Elliott from *Keep a Quiet Heart*. Copyright © 1995. Published by Servant Publications, Ann Arbor, Michigan. Used by permission.

"Life 101" by Phil Callaway from *Who Put the Skunk in the Trunk?* Published by Multnomah Publishers, Inc., Sisters, OR, © 1999. Used by permission.

"Goals for Authentic Growth" by Joe D. Batten from *New Man* magazine, March/April 1998. Used by permission.

"Five Ways to Start the New Year Right" by Liita Forsyth from *Virtue* magazine, January 2000. Used by permission of the author. Liita Forsyth has art directed three different consumer magazines and is currently an art director for Crossway Books in Wheaton, IL. She also maintains a home-based freelance design and illustration business where she lives with her husband and cat.

"Four Traits of Those Who Impact Our Lives" taken from *Growing Strong in the Seasons of Life* by Charles R. Swindoll. Copyright © 1983 by Charles R. Swindoll, Inc. Used by permission of Zondervan Publishing House.

"What Is Maturity?" by Dr. Steve Stephens, Clackamas, Oregon. Used by permission of the author.

"Vital Questions" by David Sanford, freelance writer. David Sanford is a lay pastor and vice president of publishing for the Luis Palau Evangelistic Association in Portland, Oregon. Used by permission.

"How to Put a *Wow* in Every Tomorrow" by Alice Gray, inspirational conference speaker, from her seminar, "Treasures of the Heart." Used by permission of the author.

"We Are Shaped By…" by A. W. Tozer.

"How to Lighten Up" by Ken Davis, author, adapted from the book *Lighten Up* published by Zondervan Publishing House. Used by permission of the author.

"The Optimist Creed" by Optimist International. Reprinted by permission of Optimist International, St. Louis, MO. An association of civic service clubs using the Optimist name.

VIRTUE

"A Balanced Life" from *God's Little Devotional Book*, copyright © 1995 by Honor Books, Inc., Tulsa, Oklahoma. Used by permission.

"Character and Conduct" by E. M. Bounds from *The Family Book of Christian Values*, copyright © 1995 by Christian Parenting Books.

"Good Character Is…" by St. Paul the Apostle.

"100 Positive Virtues" by Alice Gray, Dr. Steve Stephens, and John Van Diest. Used by permission of the authors.

"You Can Do It" taken from *The ABCs of Wisdom* by Ray Pritchard. Copyright © 1998, Moody Bible Institute of Chicago, Moody Press. Used by permission.

"Timeless Gifts" by Ruth Graham Bell. This article was taken from *Decision* magazine, January, 2000; © 1999 Billy Graham Evangelistic Association, used by permission, all rights reserved.

"Choosing Humility in an Arrogant World" by H. Dale Burke and Jac La Tour taken from *A Love That Never Fails*, Moody Press, copyright © 1999. Used by permission.

"Basic Manners That Teach Respect" by Bob Hostetler from *HomeLife* magazine, May 2000. Used by permission of the author. Bob Hostetler is an award-winning writer whose books include *Don't Check Your Brains at the Door* (coauthored with Josh McDowell). He lives in Hamilton, Ohio, with his wife, Robin, and two children.

"Why I Write Thank-You Notes" by Marilyn K. McAuley, copyright © 2000. Used by permission of the author. Marilyn is a freelance writer and copyeditor living in Vancouver, WA.

"The Secret List of Social Faux Pas" by Ann Platz and Susan Wales taken from *Social Graces*. Copyright © 1999 by Ann Platz and Susan Wales. Published by Harvest House Publishers, Eugene, Oregon 97402. Used by permission.

"A Virtuous Person…" by George Washington Carver.

"Three Basic Ingredients of Integrity" by Dr. Ross Campbell taken from *Relational Parenting*, Moody Press, copyright © 2000. Used by permission.

"George Washington's Rules of Civility" by George Washington.

"34 Things We Must Respect" by Dr. Steve Stephens, Clackamas, Oregon. Used by permission of the author.

"Seven Sacred Virtues" by Marilyn vos Savant from *Parade* magazine, December 5, 1999. Reprinted with permission from *Parade* and Marilyn vos Savant, copyright © 1999.

"Scout's Law" by Boy Scouts of America condensed from the *Boy Scout Handbook*. Used by permission.

FRIENDSHIP

"Why Friends Are Important" by Dr. Steve Stephens, Clackamas, Oregon. Used by permission of the author.

"10 Rules for Getting Along with People" by Norman Vincent Peale from *Time Talk*. Used by permission.

"A Friend Is One Who…" by Glenda Hotton, M.A., C.D.C., M.F.T., counselor specializing in women's issues of trauma, abuse, relationships and substance abuse in private practice in Santa Clarita, California. Used by permission of the author.

"Friendship Words" by Emilie Barnes and Donna Otto taken from *Friends of the Heart* by Emilie Barnes and Donna Otto. Copyright © 1999 by Harvest House Publishers, Eugene, Oregon 97402. Used by permission.

"The Four Promises of Forgiveness" by Ken Sande from *The Peacemaker*. Used by permission of Baker Book House, Grand Rapids, Michigan, © 1991.

"The Fine Art of Friendship" by Dr. Ted W. Engstrom condensed from *Christian Leadership Letter,* February 1986. Used by permission of the author.

"20 Questions to Ask a Friend" by Emilie Barnes and Donna Otto taken from *Friends of the Heart* by Emilie Barnes and Donna Otto. Copyright © 1999 by Harvest House Publishers, Eugene, Oregon 97402. Used by permission.

"Good Friends Are Hard to Find" by Patrick Morley taken from *The Man in the Mirror* by Patrick Morley. Copyright © 1997 by Patrick Morley. Used by permission of Zondervan Publishing House.

"Healthy Expectations of Friends" and "Unhealthy Expectations of Friends" by Glenda Hotton, M.A., C.D.C., M.F.T., counselor specializing in women's issues of trauma, abuse, relationships and substance abuse in private practice in Santa Clarita, California. Used by permission of the author.

"Antigossip Pact" by John Wesley and friends from *God's Little Devotional Book,* copyright © 1995 by Honor Books, Inc., Tulsa, Oklahoma. Used by permission.

"Proverbs on Friendship" by King Solomon selected from the Proverbs.

"10 Ideas for Staying Close When You're Far Away" by Emilie Barnes and Donna Otto taken from *Friends of the Heart* by Emilie Barnes and Donna Otto. Copyright © 1999 by Harvest House Publishers, Eugene, Oregon 97402. Used by permission.

"Fun Activities for Couple Friends" by Tricia Goyer from *HomeLife* magazine, October 1999. Used by permission.

"Being a Good Neighbor" by Tami Stephens, Clackamas, Oregon. Used by permission of the author.

HEALTH

"Stress Busters" by Alice Gray, Dr. Steve Stephens, and John Van Diest. Used by permission of the authors.

"Guidelines for Good Sleep" by American Academy of Sleep Medicine from an *AASM Wellness Booklet,* Rochester, MN. Used by permission.

"How to Keep Your Immune System Strong" by Terry Shintani, M.D., M.P.H. (nutrition Harvard University) is board certified in preventive medicine, director of integrative medicine at Coast Health Center, and author of *HawaiiDiet* (Pocket Books, 1999) and a book on "good carbohydrates" (Pocket Books, 2001).

"20 Ways to Relax" by H. Jackson Brown, Jr. condensed from *Life's Little Instruction Book* by H. Jackson Brown, Jr. and published by Rutledge Hill Press, Nashville, Tennessee. Used by permission.

"Why Laughter Is Healthy" by Dr. Steve Stephens, Clackamas, Oregon. Used by permission of the author.

"Warning Signs of Emotional Pain" by Sheri Rose Shepherd from *Fit for Excellence* (Lake Mary, FL:

Creation House, copyright © 1998, page 9). Used by permission.

"Don'ts for Emotional Fitness" by Sheri Rose Shepherd from *Fit for Excellence* (Lake Mary, FL: Creation House, copyright © 1998, page 10). Used by permission.

"Results of Anxiety" by Charles Stanley from *In Touch* magazine, January 2000, In Touch Ministries, Atlanta, GA. Used by permission.

"Avoid Getting and Doing Too Much" by Robert and Debra Bruce and Ellen Oldacre from *Standing Up Against the Odds* by Debra Fulghum Bruce and Ellen Oldacre, copyright 1999 by Concordia Publishing House. Used with permission under license number 00: 5-53.

"What Guys Need to Know about PMS" by J. Ron Eaker, M.D. condensed from *New Man* magazine, March/April 2000. Used by permission.

"Defusing Anger" by H. Dale Burke and Jac La Tour condensed from *A Love That Never Fails,* copyright © 1999, published by Moody Press, Chicago, Illinois. Used by permission.

"Top 10 Habits for Health and Vitality" by Dan Benson adapted from *THE NEW RETIREMENT: How to Secure Financial Freedom and Live Out Your Dreams* by Dan Benson. (Web site: www.NewRetirement.net) Copyright © 2000, Word Publishing, Nashville, Tennessee. All rights reserved. Used by permission of the author.

"Eating Healthy" condensed from *LifeWise* newsletter. Reprinted with permission, HOPE Publications, Kalamazoo, Michigan, (616) 343-0770.

"Guidelines for Choosing Healthy Foods" by Branda Polk condensed from *HomeLife* magazine, January 2000. Used by permission.

"Travel First-Aid Kit" by Kate Redd from *52 Ways to Make Family Travel More Enjoyable.* Reprinted by permission of Thomas Nelson Publishers from the book entitled *52 Ways to Make Family Travel More Enjoyable,* copyright 1994 by Kate Redd.

"Stay Active" by Amy Givler from *HomeLife* magazine, January 2000. © Copyright 2000 LifeWay Christian Resources of the Southern Baptist Convention. All rights reserved. Used by permission.

"How to Stop Smoking" by Amy Givler from *HomeLife* magazine, November 1999. © Copyright 1999 LifeWay Christian Resources of the Southern Baptist Convention. All rights reserved. Used by permission.

CONTENTMENT

"One Is Poor If He…" by Leroy Brownlow condensed from *A Psalm In My Heart,* © 1996 Brownlow Publishing. Used by permission.

"I Am Thankful For…" by Nancie J. Carmody from *Family Circle* magazine, November 16, 1999. Used by permission of the author.

"Joy for Today" by Goethe.

"If I Had It to Do Over Again" by John MacArthur taken from *The Family* by John MacArthur. Copyright ©1982, Moody Bible Institute of Chicago, Moody Press. Used by permission.

"Random Acts of Kindness" by Alice Gray, Dr. Steve Stephens, and John Van Diest. Used by permission of the authors.

"Tranquility" by Billy Graham from *Unto the Hills,* Billy Graham, © 1996, Word Publishing, Nashville, Tennessee. All rights reserved.

"Rules of Contentment" by E. B. Pusey.

"We All Need…" by Dr. Steve Stephens, Clackamas, Oregon. Used by permission of the author.

"20 Ways to Simplify" by Dr. Steve Stephens, Clackamas, Oregon. Used by permission of the author.

"Happiness" by John Templeton as cited in *More of…The Best of Bits & Pieces* (© 1997), published by The Economics Press, Inc., Fairfield, NJ 07004-2565; Phone: 800-526-2554. FAX: 973-227-9742. E-mail: info@epinc.com Web site: www.epinc.com.

"Life Is Hard…But God Is Good" by Sheri Rose Shepherd from *Fit for Excellence* (Lake Mary, FL: Creation House, copyright © 1998, page xi). Used by permission.

"Four Things That Bring Great Peace" by Thomas á Kempis from *The Imitation of Christ*.

MARRIAGE AND ROMANCE

"12 Actions for a Happy Marriage" by Dr. Steve Stephens, Clackamas, Oregon. Used by permission of the author.

"The Five Love Languages" by Gary Chapman from *The Five Love Languages*, copyright © 1992, published by Moody Press, Chicago, Illinois. Used by permission.

"Between a Husband and Wife" by David and Heather Kopp taken from *Unquenchable Love*. Copyright © 1999 by David and Heather Kopp. Published by Harvest House Publishers, Eugene, Oregon 97402. Used by permission.

"A Regret-Free Marriage" by Robert Jeffress from *Say Goodbye to Regret*. Published by Multnomah Publishers, Inc., Sisters, OR, © 1998. Used by permission.

"Questions to Ask Before You Say 'I Do'" by Dr. Steve Stephens, Clackamas, Oregon. Used by permission of the author.

"21 Things Every Couple Should Know" by Doug Fields taken from *365 Things Every Couple Should Know*. Copyright © 2000 by Doug Fields. Published by Harvest House Publishers, Eugene, Oregon 97402. Used by permission.

"Nine Ways to E-N-C-O-U-R-A-G-E Each Other" by Duane Storey and Sanford Kulkin from *Body and Soul*. Published by Multnomah Publishers, Inc., Sisters, OR, © 1995. Used by permission.

"50 Fun Things to Do with Your Spouse" by Dr. Steve Stephens, Clackamas, Oregon. Used by permission of the author.

"The Top 10 Mistakes Couples Make" written by Marty Crouch, copyright 1997 © Coach U. Used by permission.

"Nine Rules for Romance" by David Clark from *Men Are Clams and Women Are Crowbars*. Published by Promise Press, an imprint of Barbour Publishing, Inc., P.O. Box 719, Ulrichsville, OH 44683. Copyright © 1998.

"10 Great Romance Movies" by Dan McAuley. Used by permission of the author. Daniel McAuley is a retired school administrator and now teaches for a small private college.

"Simple Ways to Be Romantic" by Woods, Hudson, Dall, Lackland condensed from *Marriage Clues for the Clueless*. Published by Promise Press, an imprint of Barbour Publishing, Inc., P.O. Box 719, Ulrichsville, OH 44683. Copyright © 1999.

"Tips for the Romantically Challenged" by Michael Webb condensed from *New Man* magazine, March/April 2000. Used by permission.

HOME AND FINANCES

Insurance Company, New York, NY). Used by permission. All rights reserved. To order a free copy of this booklet or any of the over eighty *LifeAdvice®* pamphlets, call 1-800-METLIFE, or visit our web site at www.metlife.com.

"Qualities of a Great Baby-Sitter" by Tami Stephens, Clackamas, Oregon. Used by permission of the author.

"What Your Baby-Sitter Needs to Know" by Tami Stephens, Clackamas, Oregon. Used by permission of the author.

"Cop's Vacation Checklist" by Ken McClure, Clackamas, Oregon. Used by permission of the author.

"Six Easy Ways to Organize Your Kids' Clutter" by Faith Tibbetts McDonald from *Virtue* magazine, March/April 1998. Used by permission of the author.

"22 Items to Always Carry in Your Car" by Al Gray, Redmond, Oregon. Used by permission of the author.

"Create a Family Craft Box" by Tricia Goyer condensed from *HomeLife* magazine, January 2000. © Copyright 2000 LifeWay Christian Resources of the Southern Baptist Convention. All rights reserved. Used by permission.

TEENS

"10 Gifts for Your Teens" by Susan Alexander Yates condensed from *How to Like the Ones You Love*. Used by permission of Baker Book House, Grand Rapids, Michigan, © 2000.

"How Well Do You Know Your Teenager?" by Miriam Neff, B.A., M.A., Northwestern University, counselor in public high school, mother of four, author, and speaker, condensed from *FamilyLife Today* radio program. Used by permission of the author.

"How to Motivate Your Teen" by Gary and Anne Marie Ezzo from *Reaching the Heart of Your Teen*. Published by Multnomah Publishers, Inc., Sisters, OR, © 1997. Used by permission.

"Kids Who Resist Peer Pressure Have…" by Don S. Otis condensed from *Teach Your Children Well*. Used by permission of Baker Book House, Grand Rapids, Michigan, © 2000.

"Five Secrets of Parenting Teens" by Ted Haggard and John Bolin taken from *Confident Parents, Exceptional Teens* by Ted Haggard and John Bolin. Copyright © 1999 by Ted Haggard and John Bolin. Used by permission of Zondervan Publishing House.

"How to Raise Sexually Pure Kids" by Tim and Beverly LaHaye from *Raising Sexually Pure Kids*. Published by Multnomah Publishers, Inc., Sisters, OR, © 1998. Used by permission.

"Four Ways to Stay Sexually Pure" by Robert Jeffress from *Saying Goodbye to Regret*. Published by Multnomah Publishers, Inc., Sisters, OR, © 1998. Used by permission.

"Qualities of a Good Teen Friend" by Don S. Otis from *Teach Your Children Well*. Used by permission of Baker Book House, Grand Rapids, Michigan, © 2000.

"Teen Group-Dating Ideas" by Jimmy Hester condensed from *HomeLife* magazine, February 2000. © Copyright 2000 LifeWay Christian Resources of the Southern Baptist Convention. All rights reserved. Used by permission.

"How to Teach Respect" by Bob Hostetler from *HomeLife* magazine, May 2000. Used by permission of the author. Bob Hostetler is an award-winning writer whose books include *Don't Check Your Brains at the Door* (coauthored with Josh McDowell). He lives in Hamilton, Ohio, with his wife, Robin, and two children.

"When Your Teen Fails" by Gary Chapman condensed from *The Five Love Languages of Teenagers*, Northfield Publishing, a division of Moody Press, copyright © 2000. Used by permission.

"Minimize Materialism" by Don S. Otis condensed from *Teach Your Children Well*. Used by permission of Baker Book House, Grand Rapids, Michigan, © 2000.

"Warning Signs That My Child Is Headed for Trouble" by Dr. Greg Cynaumon from *Helping Single Parents with Troubled Kids*. Used by permission of the author.

"Warning Signs of Teens Headed for Violent Behavior" by Mark A. Tabb condensed from *HomeLife* magazine, November 1999. © Copyright 1999 LifeWay Christian Resources of the Southern Baptist Convention. All rights reserved. Used by permission.

"10 Commandments for Teenagers" by Ted Haggard and John Bolin taken from *Confident Parents, Exceptional Teens* by Ted Haggard and John Bolin. Copyright © 1999 by Ted Haggard and John Bolin. Used by permission of Zondervan Publishing House.

FAMILY LIFE

"Children Learn What They Live" by Dorothy Law Nolte excerpted from the book *Children Learn What They Live*. Copyright © 1998 by Dorothy Law Nolte and Rachel Harris. The poem "Children Learn What They Live" on page vi copyright © 1972 by Dorothy Law Nolte. Used by permission of Workman Publishing Co., Inc., New York. All rights reserved.

"Teaching the ABCs to Your Children" by Glenda Hotton, M.A., C.D.C., M.F.T., counselor specializing in women's issues of trauma, abuse, relationships and substance abuse in private practice in Santa Clarita, California. Used by permission of the author.

"Helping Your Child Succeed" by Gary Smalley from *The Key to Your Child's Heart*, Gary Smalley, © 1984, Word Publishing, Nashville, Tennessee. All rights reserved.

"Every Parent Should Ask..." by Dr. John C. Maxwell, Founder, The INJOY Group (Web site: www.injoy.com) from *Breakthrough Parenting*. Used by permission of the author.

"25 Ways to Help Your Child Do Better in School" by Jan Dargatz from *52 Ways to Help Your Child Do Better in School*. Reprinted by permission of Thomas Nelson Publishers from the book entitled *52 Ways to Help Your Child Do Better in School*, copyright 1993 by Jan Dargatz.

"13 Ways to Get Your Child to Read" by Doris Howard. Used by permission of the author.

"Kids Online" by Donna Rice Hughes from *Kids Online*. Used by permission of Baker Book House, Grand Rapids, Michigan, © 1998.

"Showing Respect for Your Child" by Ron Hutchcraft taken from *Five Needs Your Child Must Have Met at Home* by Ron Hutchcraft. Copyright © 1995 by Ron Hutchcraft. Used by permission of Zondervan Publishing House.

"25 Ways to Enjoy Your Family" by Tim Kimmel condensed from *Little House on the Freeway*. Published by Multnomah Publishers, Inc., Sisters, OR, © 1987, 1994. Used by permission.

"Three Ways to Keep Family Boundaries" by Dr. Mary Manz Simon condensed from *Christian Parenting Today* magazine, March/April 2000. Used by permission of the author. Dr. Simon is a nationally recognized speaker, bestselling author, and consultant on the children's marketplace. Dr. Simon also hosts the nationally syndicated daily radio program, *Front Porch Parenting*.

"Tips to Custom-Fit Your Parenting" by Dottie G. Bachtell from *Today's Christian Woman* magazine, March/April 2000. Used by permission of the author. Dottie G. Bachtell works for Marketplace Ministries as an Industrial Chaplain in Longview, Texas. She is a freelance writer, speaker, and homemaker. She and husband, Charlie, have two sons.

"The 10 Commandments of Grandparenting" by Dr. Larry Keefauver from *Hugs for Grandparents*, published by Howard Publishing. Used by permission. Larry Keefauver, D.Min., the senior editor of *Ministries Today* magazine and copastor of The Gathering Place Worship Center, Lake Mary, Florida, has authored *Hugs for Grandparents*; *Lord, I Wish My Husband Would Pray with Me*; and more than forty other books.

"Good Times with Grandparents" by Cynthia Sumner from *MomSense*, Spring 1996. Used by permission of MOPS International.

"Golden Moments in a Child's Day" by Ron Hutchcraft taken from *Five Needs Your Child Must Have Met at Home* by Ron Hutchcraft. Copyright © 1995 by Ron Hutchcraft. Used by permission of Zondervan Publishing House.

"Principles of Parenting" by Jani Ortlund condensed from *Fearlessly Feminine*. Published by Multnomah Publishers, Inc., Sisters, OR, copyright © 2000. Used by permission of the author.

"Starting Your Child on Good Health" by Dr. Loraine Stern, M.D. condensed from *Woman's Day* magazine, January 4, 2000. Used by permission of the author. Dr. Stern is an associate clinical professor at UCLA Department of Pediatrics, Fellow, American Academy of Pediatrics.

"Building Relationships with Your Married Kids" by David and Claudia Arp adapted from *The Second Half of Marriage* (Zondervan, 1996). Used by permission of the authors. David and Claudia Arp, founders of Marriage Alive, are educators, national speakers and seminar leaders, and authors of numerous books including *10 Great Dates* and *The Second Half of Marriage* (both Zondervan). Website: www.marriagealive.com. E-mail: TheArps@marriagealive.com.

"10 Best Indoor Games Ever" by Jerry and Patti MacGregor taken from *Family Times*. Copyright © 1999 by Jerry and Patti MacGregor. Published by Harvest House Publishers, Eugene, Oregon 97402. Used by permission.

FAMILY LOVE

"A Parent's Commitment" by Gary Smalley and John Trent from *Leaving the Light On*. Published by Multnomah Publishers, Inc., Sisters, OR, © 1991. Used by permission.

"25 Simple Ways to Tell Your Child 'I Love You'" by Jan Dargatz from *52 Simple Ways to Tell Your Child "I Love You."* Reprinted by permission of Thomas Nelson Publishers from the book entitled *52 Simple Ways to Tell Your Child "I Love You,"* copyright 1991 by Jan Dargatz.

"A Parent's Daily Prayer Guide" by Don and Sue Myers condensed from *Real FamilyLife* magazine, March/April 2000. Permission granted by Don Myers, director-at-large, Campus Crusade for Christ International.

"Ways to Make Your Mom Feel Special" by Charlotte Adelsperger. Portions of this article were taken from *Focus on the Family "Clubhouse"* magazine, May 2000; copyright by Charlotte Adelsperger, used by permission of the author.

"Ways to Honor Your Dad" by John Van Diest. Used by permission of the author.

"Affirming Your Children" by Elisa Morgan and Carol Kuykendall taken from *What Every Child Needs* by Elisa Morgan and Carol Kuykendall. Copyright © 1997 by MOPS International, Inc. Used by permission of Zondervan Publishing House.

"Messages That Last a Lifetime" by William Sears, Martha Sears, Joyce Warman, et al., condensed from *Parent Project: Tools for Godly Parenting.* Copyright © 1999 LifeWay Press, Nashville, Tennessee. Used by permission.

"10 Gifts to Give Your Children" by T. Berry Brazelton, M.D. Adapted from *10 Gift to Give Your Children*, copyright © 1998 by T. Berry Brazelton, M.D. Originally appeared in *Family Circle*. This usage granted by permission of Lescher & Lescher, Ltd.

"Maximize Your Grandparenting Skills" by John Van Diest. Used by permission of the author.

"I Remember Grandma and Grandpa Because…" by Pat Van Diest. Used by permission of the author.

"Traits of a Loving Family" by Dolores Curran from *Traits of a Healthy Family*; Harper San Francisco; 1985. Used by permission of the author.

"Four Foundation Stones of Parental Love" by Dr. Ross Campbell taken from *Relational Parenting* by Dr. Ross Campbell, Moody Press, copyright © 2000. Used by permission.

"Keep Communication Open with Your Child" by Stephen Arterburn from *Parents Guide to Top 10 Dangers Teens Face* by Stephen Arterburn and Jim Burns, a Focus on the Family book published by Tyndale House Publishers. All rights reserved. International copyright secured. Used by permission.

"Six Questions to Get Your Kids Talking" by John Trent, Ph.D. condensed from *Christian Parenting Today* magazine, March/April 2000. Used by permission of the author.

"Giving Love to Children" by Donna Otto taken from *The Gentle Art of Mentoring*. Copyright © 1997 by Donna Otto. Published by Harvest House Publishers, Eugene, Oregon 97402. Used by permission.

"Bolstering Your Child's Confidence" by Karen Dockrey from *Parenting: Questions Women Ask.* Published by Multnomah Publishers, Inc., Sisters, OR, © 1992. Used by permission.

WISDOM

"Seven Lessons for Living" by Grandma Sinclair taken from *Well Done!* by Dave Thomas. Copyright © 1994 by R. David Thomas. Used by permission of Zondervan Publishing House.

"Wise Sayings My Mother Taught Me" by Nola Bertelson, Salem, Oregon. Used by permission of the author.

"A Father's Advice" by Bob Welch taken from *A Father for All Seasons*. Copyright © 1998 by Bob Welch. Published by Harvest House Publishers, Eugene, Oregon 97402. Used by permission.

"Do Good" by St. Paul the Apostle selected from Romans.

"Life" by Percy Bysshe Shelley.

"10 Rules to Live By" selected from *A Better Way to Live* by Og Mandino, copyright © 1990 by Og Mandino. Used by permission of Bantam Books, a division of Random House, Inc.

"Kids Say the Wisest Things" by Phil Callaway from *Who Put the Skunk in the Trunk?* Published by Multnomah Publishers, Inc., Sisters, OR, © 1999. Used by permission.

"The Wisdom of Abraham Lincoln" by Abraham Lincoln.

"10 Secrets to Ageless Living" by Kelly Ferrin from *What's Age Got to Do with It?*, copyright © 1999, published by ALTI Publishing, San Diego, California. Used by permission.

"Practical Words of a Philosopher" by Baltasar Gracian.

"Vanity" by Thomas á Kempis from *The Imitation of Christ*.

"Seize the Day..." by Bruce Bickel and Stan Jantz adapted from *God Is in the Small Stuff: And It All Matters*. Published by Promise Press, an imprint of Barbour Publishing, Inc., P.O. Box 719, Ulrichsville, OH 44683. Copyright © 1998. Used by permission.

"12 Lessons Worth Repeating" by Marian Wright Edelman from *The Measure of Our Success* by Marian Wright Edelman © 1992 by Marian Wright Edelman. Reprinted by permission of Beacon Press, Boston.

"Fear and Faith" by Phil Callaway from *Who Put the Skunk in the Trunk?* Published by Multnomah Publishers, Inc., Sisters, OR, © 1999. Used by permission.

"Handbook of Wisdom" Bruce and Cheryl Bickel and Stan and Karin Jantz from *Life's Little Handbook of Wisdom*. Published by Barbour Publishing, Inc., P.O. Box 719, Ulrichsville, OH 44683. Copyright © 1992. Used by permission.

LISTS TO LIVE BY FOR EVERY CARING FAMILY

compiled by Alice Gray, Steve Stephens, and John Van Diest

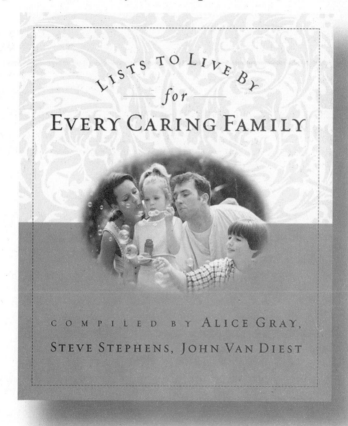

Success Strategies of Families that Flourish

Moms and Dads will welcome the loving, insightful, and to-the-point wisdom found in *Lists to Live By for Every Caring Family*. Each of the eighty lists, compiled by three successful and respected authors, offers encouragement and tender advice for today's parenting challenges. This isn't another trivia book; *Lists* provides new inspiration on how to love, teach, understand, uplift, and communicate with children on topics such as "Helping Your Child Succeed," "Praying for Your Children," and "Four Ways to Encourage Your Kids." Parents will cherish each nugget of truth in this latest timeless collection of *Lists to Live By*.

ISBN 1-57673-999-6

LISTS TO LIVE BY FOR EVERY MARRIED COUPLE

compiled by Alice Gray, Steve Stephens, and John Van Diest

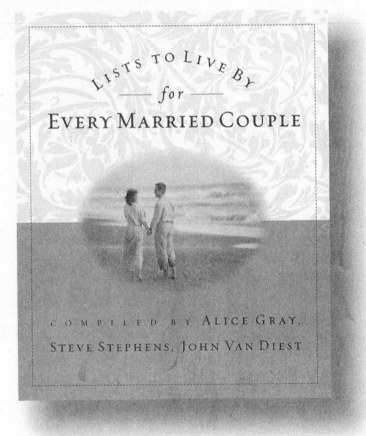

Love and Logic for the Happy Couple

On-the-go wives and husbands who seek a burst of inspiration or encouragement for their relationship will find just what they need in *Lists to Live By for Every Married Couple*. Approximately eighty lists, compiled by three respected authors, provide couples with insights on love, communication, romance, fun, forgiveness, making memories, and more. More than another trivia book, *Lists* offers tender, romantic, and wise ways to bring new life to marriage in a popular, easy-to-read format. This latest collection of *Lists to Live By* is filled with gems of inspiration and timeless truths that married couples will treasure and use for a lifetime.

ISBN 1-57673-998-8